A
Lonely
Journey

CC Thompson
Journey Publish LLC

A Lonely Journey
Compiled by CC Thompson
Published by Journey Publish LLC
P.O. Box 881
Appleton, WI 54912-0881
www.JourneyPublish.com
JourneyPublish@gmail.com

Copyright © 2018 by Journey Publish LLC
All rights reserved. No part of this book may be reproduced, stored in, or introduced into a retrieval system, or transmitted to any form, or by any means to include electronic, mechanical, photocopying, recording, or otherwise without the prior written permission of the individual authors.

This book should not be used as a substitute for the advice of medical or legal professionals.

First printing, May 2018
Printed in the United States of America
Library of Congress Control Number: 2018904271
ISBN: 978-1-7322069-0-8
ePUB ISBN: 978-1-7322069-1-5
Cover photo credit Webtech.com
10 9 8 7 6 5 4 3 2 1

DEDICATION

This book is dedicated to the amazing caregivers who have joined together to share their experiences in this book so other caregivers can benefit from this sharing and that family members, friends, co-workers and employers can better understand the journey of a dementia caregiver.

SHARING THE JOURNEY

Disclaimer...i

Introduction..iii

Am I Okay..1

And So Our Journey Began....................................5

Can I Say This Out Loud......................................27

Caregiver Stress..31

Dear Dementia..35

Dementia Has Taught Me....................................39

Diagnosis Process...43

God Has My Back...51

Have You Seen My Spouse..................................53

How Can You Help Me..57

How Far I Have Journeyed..................................61

Humor Is Important...67

I Am Tired..71

I Feel Blessed...75

I Highly Recommend This	77
John	81
Long Long Journey	91
Losing John	113
Memories of Mom	123
My Grandmothers	129
My Heroes	135
My Journey	139
My Life As A Caregiver	149
My Sons Caregiver	153
Sense of Purpose	157
Some Days	159
Support	163
Support Groups Are Priceless	165
The D Word	169
This Is Not The Retirement We Planned	173
Time Stood Still	177
Traveling	181
What I Have Learned	185
What I Miss Most	201

What Is Dementia...205

Who Is Looking Back At Me............................209

You Are Not Alone...211

Thank You..215

Afterword...217

Disclaimer..219

A LONLEY JOURNEY

DISCLAIMER

These journeys are written and shared by caregivers in their own words, not by medical or legal professionals.

Any information shared in this book is not intended to be nor should it be interpreted as medical or legal advice.

Medical and legal questions or concerns should be directed to your medical and legal professionals.

A LONLEY JOURNEY

INTRODUCTION

The title, *"A Lonely Journey,"* was selected because at first the journey does appear very lonely, but as we come together and share our experiences, the road no longer feels like *"A Lonely Journey."*

A heartfelt gratitude to all the wonderful amazing caregivers who, in their own words, shared their journeys and made this book possible. We have respected the privacy of those caregivers that have requested to remain anonymous. It is the intent that all caregivers find support and solace in the sharing and reading of these journeys.

As each submission is unique to itself, there are no numerated chapters. It was difficult to decide what order to arrange the submissions in, so they are arranged in alphabetical order based on their titles. The alphabetizing of the journeys also allows the ability to flip through the book and easily find a journey you may want to refer to later.

God's continued blessings to all of you on your journeys!

CC Thompson

AM I OKAY

This may sound like a funny title, but there are many days that I wonder if I need a caregiver.

Have you as a caregiver ever asked yourself this question too? I do often. Maybe too often.

I have caught myself ready to leave the house only to find I still have my pajama bottoms on. I have actually been in public with two different colored shoes on. Some days I struggle for common words myself. Some days I think that I should be the loved one and my spouse should be the caregiver. I hope by now you are laughing with me and not at me!

My doctor tells me not to worry. I still do. Supposedly it is not that uncommon for caregivers to have these moments? As caregivers we have so much on our minds.

It's funny how someone can ask me about my spouse and I can tell them just about every little detail of his day or even yesterday, but when the conversation turns to myself my mind seems to go blank.

Sometimes people will ask my opinion about something and in all honesty many times I have to stop to think about how I actually do feel.

I feel like I have become one with my husband. My life is his life and I no longer have my own life. It's not that I really mind. It's just that I am finding that I don't seem to have a life. My own life has disappeared.

I am told as a caregiver I need to get out more and to take care of myself. Sounds easy, but it isn't. As a caregiver where do I find the time for me? When he naps, I try to get things caught up around the house or possibly a short nap for myself, which seldom happens.

My New Year resolution again was to take more time for myself, but already several months into the year, I find I have failed again. Perhaps just wearing makeup again may give me a mental boost that I need.

There are so many things I would love to do. Go for a walk. Read a book. Watch TV. Just sit in silence. But he needs me. Somedays I liken him to a two year old and some days he is more like an 8 year old. I hate to talk that way about him, but it is how it feels. Most days I feel I have a toddler.

So, I guess, it is no wonder that I would ask if I am okay. After all, my brain is not getting any younger either. I will keep trying to take better care of myself so I can take care of him for as long as he needs me to. Forgive me if I have offended anyone.

—Doing Okay

Myth: As we age it is normal to have dementia

AND SO OUR JOURNEY BEGAN

When did our journey begin? Looking back I think the journey begins without you even realizing the journey has begun. When did the journey begin is a question that could have so many responses. I recall the first signs of our journey surfaced five years before we were finally given a correct diagnosis. And so I believe this is where our journey began.

I noticed my spouse, Ann, who had created a successful business over the previous 25 years, seemed to be unable to organize her day and appeared to be running in circles and accomplishing very little.

At first, I mentioned my concerns to close friends and they would laugh and say, "Tony, we are all getting older. It's normal." My concerns were

A LONELY JOURNEY

repeatedly shut down and dismissed even though I was still troubled by the signs.

Ann and I first met when I was 14 and she was 16, but we did not date until years later. Ann was always extremely well-mannered in the 34 years I had known her at this point. A trait that I highly valued in her. However, I started to notice oddities with her manners such as taking a dinner roll when we were dining out and then putting it back after it was on her plate because she decided she didn't want it after all. Another time, she kept scraping her crackers in the cheese spread that was at the table instead of putting the cheese on her plate and using a knife to spread the cheese on her cracker.

One incident I may never forget was when we were entertaining at our home and one of the guests mentioned to her that she had butter on the side of her little finger. There was a considerable amount and Ann promptly wiped the butter on her pants.

The look on our guests' faces was quite disturbing and I am sure my face looked just as surprised.

When I asked Ann about the incident later she responded with, "That is what you do. You wipe it off." The Ann I knew would have used her napkin.

Over the next few years, I saw Ann get more and more frustrated as she struggled to keep up with her business. I am sure her frustration was due to her lack of productivity. But she continued to deny any issues and would inform me it was because she was so swamped with work. I was working full-time, but was also taking on more and more of her work that her staff could not handle.

Much to my dismay, I found as I was taking on more of her workload, she was now spending more time with a morning and noon social group of women and even taking afternoon naps. She would go to bed at 9 p.m. and I would be up considerably later finishing her work for the day.

We had a discussion about the importance of my sleep too. This is when I started to realize she was no longer capable of doing her paperwork or organizing her day. Socializing and naps were her day.

It was now four years later after I first suspected Ann was struggling. Our friends and now family were still not convinced anything was wrong as she was "just getting older and it was perfectly normal." I would respond with, "But I am the one who lives with her and I should know."

I wanted to get Ann to a doctor, but I wondered what do I say? My spouse is 54 and forgetful? I have forgetful moments too. I am a bit younger. So will I be like her in a few years and find out it is normal? I would struggle with these questions nightly as I went to sleep.

Although Ann was complaining of being quite tired, one Sunday she insisted we go for an afternoon ride and also dine out that evening. I was tired, but at her insistence I agreed and she agreed to drive. We were on familiar roads and I looked down at my phone to check a text and looked up in surprise to see that we were on the wrong side of the road heading for the ditch. I screamed, "What are you doing?" Her head was down and her eyes were half closed. At that moment she looked up and instead of hitting the brakes she put the gas pedal to the floor which resulted in snapping off a road sign. Ann continued to use the gas pedal instead of the brake as we went from side to side of the road with tires squealing. We finally came to a stop with our vehicle spinning around and now pointed in the opposite direction on the wrong side of the road.

Ann then drove into a driveway and I started to call 911. She screamed, "What are you doing?" I told her we were just in an accident and we need to call for the police to come and write up a report. Ann asked me if I was crazy and stated you don't call 911 and started to back up and was apparently planning on leaving the scene even though people were now gathered in their yards due to the squealing tires.

This behavior was so unlike Ann. We had not been drinking and it made no sense why she was upset that I was calling 911. Our vehicle was still drivable, but we had considerable damage on the driver's side. I continued to call 911 much to her displeasure.

I am so thankful to God when I look back at that day. We were the last vehicle through the stoplight. The speed limit was just going from 25 mph to 45 mph. There was no traffic coming at us which allowed our vehicle to go from side to side on the road without hitting another vehicle. We were told later there were two motorcyclist who saw what was happening and pulled onto the side of the road. I am so thankful they had the presence of mind to pull over and that we did not hit them. Much to my surprise Ann also insisted that we still continue on to go out to eat instead of heading home which would have been my choice.

When Ann and I talked about it later, we were both surprised to hear that both our thoughts ad been "so this is how it is going to end" and that due to our faith we had both felt at peace with it.

Two days later I told my mother about the accident. She suggested Ann may have had a TIA (mini stroke). WOW! I felt I now had a reason I could get Ann to the doctor and perhaps this may be what has been causing some issues. Ann fought me on the idea as she felt she fell asleep, even though the accident happened early afternoon. I made the appointment anyway, got off work, went home and told her to get in the car which surprisingly she did and I drove to the appointment.

At the doctor's office we were told it wasn't possible to be able to tell if she had a TIA as it had been a week. The doctor did suggest possible sleep apnea and an appointment for testing was arranged, but the results were negative.

Two weeks later, as I was getting into bed about 10:00 pm, after a busy night, Ann came into the bedroom and said she felt strange and wanted to go to the emergency room. How strange! Ann was asking to see a doctor? I jumped up and got dressed. We had a 45 minute drive to the hospital. When we arrived, the receptionist asked Ann her name and what was wrong. To my surprise, Ann's words were now slurred and she wasn't making any sense. Again, I am thinking TIA!

Tests at the ER showed Ann had toxic poisoning due to a high level in her system of a medication she had been taking. The doctor attributed it to the excessive heat we had been having and dehydration causing a concentration of the medication in her system.

Her blood pressure was extremely high. Ann was given medication to lower her blood pressure and it immediately put her into a snoring sleep. I was told later it was fortunate we got to the ER as soon as we did as she would have had a heart attack due to the high blood pressure.

Ann, of course, was admitted and I was told to go home and rest as she was stable and due to the medication she was given she was expected to sleep through the night. When I arrived the next day, I was told Ann was moved to the behavioral health floor as she was having some issues.

Ann was released from the hospital after two weeks, but as we were leaving I was shocked when staff handed me six prescription slips that I had to get filled. This was the start of a series of hospital stays for Ann for the next year and a half.

The worst part of all these doctor visits and hospital stays was that HIPAA had recently been made law. So I was being repeatedly told by doctors that they cannot share information and results with me. What? How can I help her if they don't tell me what is going on? I learned Ann had more rights that I did especially due to her behavioral health stay and medications. This was all compounded by the fact that her new medications seemed to be making her paranoid and not wanting to sign any consent forms.

One night I was awoken at 3 a.m. by the sound of Ann sobbing in our family room. I went downstairs and asked her what was wrong. She didn't seem to know. I, of course, got Ann in to see a doctor the next day.

Ann was admitted again for behavioral health care and a week later sent home with more medication.

Ann's behavior continued to escalate and finally a three party petition had to be filed so now the county was involved and a caseworker was assigned.

I told the caseworker of my concerns and suspicions of early onset dementia. She stated the doctors didn't feel that was her problem.

In October, Ann wasn't taking her medication so the county now placed her in a county behavioral health hospital where she spent six weeks. I was told not to visit as they felt it would make things worse and that she was not talking favorably about me.

After a few weeks I called and requested a visit and was told by the hospital social worker that it was about time I called and questioned why I haven't visited Ann. WOW! Talk about poor communication.

A LONELY JOURNEY

Ann was very cordial when I visited. I brought along some photos I had just received and much to my surprise she wasn't able to identify people in the photo including our son.

I again was being told nothing about her condition as releases were not signed. I had to get a judge to order the doctors to release information to me.

The doctor very coldly told me that it was discovered that Ann had an arachnoid (clear liquid filled) cyst in the back lining of her brain and that they needed to operate to drain the cyst, but Ann would not sign the forms.

Why would you ask a behavioral health patient to sign such a form when they are heavily medicated? How can that be legal? She was clearly cognitively impaired.

The doctor went on to tell me that before they knew about the cysts her diagnosis was incurable mental illness and they were going to recommend that Ann live in a care facility. The doctor also advised me that I should get my affairs in order as Ann did not have long to live.

Of course, when I was finally able to take Ann home a week later, I was given more prescription slips. Ann was now taking 15 pills a day plus a weekly injection to control her moods.

Thankfully, at this time, my manager at work allowed me to work part-time and adjust my hours as needed.

The person I brought home was not my spouse. Ann was falling out of bed and crawling on her hands and knees to get to the bathroom. She would smear her feces in the bathroom because she was so over medicated that she had no idea she didn't have toilet paper in her hand. She would soil herself. She was unable to shower as she could barely stand and although she could bathe, it was a major struggle to get her back out and I literally had to pull her over the side and onto the floor. Ann was unable to even operate the remote for the TV and it wasn't unusual to see her staring at a blue screen because she pushed a wrong button on the remote.

Ann spent most her time sleeping and would sleep for three days straight after her weekly injection. When the local doctors first saw the prescribed injection dose, they said it had to be a mistake as they had never seen a dose that high prescribed, but when they called to verify the dose they were told it was not a mistake.

I was unable to alter any of the medications Ann was taking because she was still under a court order and local doctors were unable to make changes as well. At this point, Ann is now using a walker due to frequent falls.

Still looking for answers, I contacted Mayo Clinic for help. Initially our request was declined.

I suspect due to all the medical records were stating it was a mental health issue. I appealed and gave examples of her behavior and they agreed to put us on their waiting list.

Since I was now eligible for early retirement, I decided it was the time to retire.

The court order was finally removed that Spring. The local doctors were now able to make changes with her medications and I was able to get the injections stopped. In order to change her medications, the doctors said she would have to be in the hospital again for observation while the changes were made.

The plan was to take away medications, however, she came home with more prescription slips and Ann was now up to 22 pills a day. I was told Ann is very sensitive to medications and the additional meds were due to side effects.

I threw out the new medication and decided we

had nothing to lose at this point. Ann was using a walker and we were still understanding that she didn't have long to live. So I slowly discontinued her medications myself. I am not recommending that anyone else discontinues medications, but again I felt I had nothing to lose at this point.

I was also now in the process of dissolving the business and selling our home as well as preparing to be a widower and meeting with financial advisors and lawyers.

Ann improved over the next few months and she was stable enough to start driving locally again, but yet had some noticeable cognitive issues.

It took a year, but thankfully, Ann was now at the top of the list for Mayo Clinic and off we went for what we thought was a one hour appointment. Our expected one hour visit turned into five days of outpatient specialists and tests. It was amazing! Different specialists met with us for four hours each day! Each day we had the full attention of our "specialist of the day" as if they had nothing else to do.

The four hours were tiring and grueling for myself as we answered the doctors' questions. I can only imagine how difficult it was for Ann.

On the second day, our "specialist of the day" told us that three of the medications Ann was on he would NEVER recommend combining and stated no wonder Ann does not remember the past almost two years. If only I could forget!

At this point we had no actual diagnosis yet, but I had shared my suspicions of early onset dementia. I was then informed that some of the medications prescribed and taken by Ann should never be given to a person with dementia as they could cause further issues.

On our final day at Mayo Clinic, Ann was given four hours of neurological testing. We had to wait several weeks for the results, but I was finally relieved to see early onset dementia NOS (not otherwise specified) in the diagnosis. Ann was 57 when she was finally medically diagnosed. I was elated, but heartbroken. But at least now I felt I knew what direction to proceed.

Ann, currently, still insists she does not have dementia and says "there is nothing wrong with me," but yet she takes her medication and doesn't put up a fuss when she has a medical appointment. Ann does refuse to get involved with any memory cafes or groups other than an occasional memory bus trip. I am so thankful for the local caring businesses that make these wonderful bus trips possible for the loved ones and their caregivers.

Last year, we had to change primary physicians for a year due to insurance issues. On our final visit last year, the physician told me that Ann was too young to have dementia. Whoa! That's why they call it early onset! Definitely not knowledgeable about dementia. Thankfully we were able to return the first of the year to our previous primary physician who was so helpful through our nightmare journey.

Several MRIs have been performed over the past years for Ann's cyst, but there has been no growth over the years and doctors feel it is no longer a concern. Doctors concluded she may have been born with this cyst or it may have formed when she was struck by a car when she was young.

Friends have totally disappeared for Ann. I and the TV are her daily interaction. I guess the saying is true that in hard times you find out who your real friends are. I have lost several close friends as well, but through this journey I have met new friends who are on the same caregiving journey as I am. Sharing with these wonderful new friends makes me feel "normal." I have learned not to share Ann's condition outside any dementia group as I have found to my surprise people then treat us BOTH differently. Dementia is not contagious!

It's funny how friends disappear and family become distant when they hear the word dementia. It only makes the journey lonelier for the caregiver and their loved one.

I realize our journey is far from over. Dementia continues to slowly creep in and eat away. Dementia is a cruel disease in that it allows good days which tricks the caregiver into believing everything will be okay and the dementia is "cured." All you really can do is enjoy the good days while you still have them.

There currently is no cure. Only medications which are believed to help slow down the process. How do you compare to know if it really is slowing the process? Caregivers have no choice, but to trust that the medications are helping.

AND SO OUR JOURNEY BEGAN

I am sharing this story in hopes that your loved one and you, as a caregiver, will never have to experience what we did. We endured almost two years of unnecessary extreme stress in search of a diagnosis when my suspicions were correct in the first place.

Even to this day we have friends and family who are still in denial that Ann has any type of dementia. I always say they need to spend a week with Ann and then talk to me about it. Dementia is not easily detected in just spending a few hours with someone.

One friend recently commented that Ann has a remarkable memory and can remember so many events that happened in high school. I explained to the friend that is how dementia works. Past events can be vivid, but recent events not so much. The friend still wasn't convinced.

I can't help but wonder what additional damage

all those unnecessary medications did. Medications Ann was given because doctors would not listen to me and yet they were way off base on what Ann's diagnosis really was. Thank God for the caring experts at Mayo Clinic.

—Tony

CAN I SAY THIS OUT LOUD

I am not perfect, but I try my best.

Some days I want to scream and some days I do, but in private. Some days I want to just have a good cry, and some days I do, but in private.

I just wish I could be a better me. It's not that I am in any way physically or mentally abusive to my spouse, by any means. It's my thoughts that I keep to myself that bother me.

I recently shared my feelings with two other caregivers and found I am not alone with my feelings. So that is why I am sharing with you that I am not a perfect caregiver.

As much as I love my spouse, some days I wish he were gone. Partly from my own selfishness and partly because it is hard to see him struggle. I feel he must be praying himself for his struggle to end.

He has always taken great care of me and was quick to ensure I would be taken care of after he is gone. That only adds to my guilt feelings.

In reviewing what I have written here, I realize that I struggle to use the "d" words and have chosen "gone." Is it because I am not ready to face reality? I like to think that it is my belief in the afterlife that makes me choose the word "gone" instead.

I do have to admit that I haven't given up. The journey is not over for us, but I do pray daily for guidance and patience to make me a better caregiver. I feel it is the guilt in me that doesn't allow me to pat myself on the back and say, "Today you did a great job!"

I have come to realize that as caregivers we need to work on our guilt feelings and allow ourselves to feel good about what we do each day. I am learning to set daily goals that are small in order to keep from disappointing myself. Most days my goal is simply to get my spouse to smile.

I usually find at the end of the day, if he had a good day, then I had a good day as well. As they say, "one day at a time."

Pat yourself on the back today or better yet wrap your arms around yourself and give yourself an awesome hug because you deserve it! You are an awesome caregiver!

—Humbly Submitted

*Caregiving is not
for sissies*

CAREGIVER STRESS

I have heard the words "Caregiver Stress" many times in my life over many years. Those words didn't mean too much to me until a few years ago when I became a caregiver for a family member.

I didn't understand at that time what those words actually meant until I experienced being a caregiver. I am now ashamed to say I was apathetic since it didn't apply to me. I now understand the meaning of those two words more than I care to.

I have experienced stress in my life, but I would say the stress was situational and periodical. Being a caregiver has given me a new insight into a new kind of stress. A 24/7 stress.

There may be small moments of joy or a glimpse of a smile, but the stress of caregiving is always in the room. The "what if" is always there. What if they fall? What if they decide to leave the house while I am out of the room or while I am asleep? What if? What if? What if? I never knew I could think of so many "what ifs." So many "what ifs" that I never used to even think about.

As a caregiver it is difficult to nap or sleep at night. It is difficult to get good rest. You take precautions to prevent something from happening, but yet you worry that you haven't done enough.

Personally, I would say that caregiving is the greatest stress that I have experienced so far in my life. I imagine there are greater stresses in this world, but this is the greatest for me, so far.

I have learned that caregiving is not for sissies. Caregiving is for super heroes. Caregiving takes lots of energy, determination, advocacy, patience, compassion, dedication and love. All of which I have found an abundance of only because I needed to. I had someone dependent on me and I had no other choice but to dig deep and find these traits. I truly amazed myself and in looking back being a caregiver has made me a better person.

I know caregiving has lots of stressful days and even weeks, but somehow we, as caregivers, pick ourselves up each and every day ready to take on whatever the day will bring us.

Remember that as strong as we are, we still have to take care of ourselves so we can continue to be awesome caregivers. Onward super heroes!

—Super Caregiver

A LONELY JOURNEY

*Have you ever wanted to
write a letter to dementia
and let it know how you feel?*

DEAR DEMENTIA

Dear Dementia:

It is about time that I write you a letter. This letter is long overdue.

You crept into my loved one's life without asking. Then you came into my life without asking. You are an uninvited guest at our home.

Do you enjoy watching us struggle? Did you enjoy watching us trying to put all the pieces together? Trying to figure out what was going on? Did you enjoy seeing me cry?

Did you enjoy tearing our family apart? Did you enjoy the conflict and the denial by family members? Did you enjoy watching our friends slowly disappear?

Did you enjoy watching me struggle trying to

A LONELY JOURNEY

keep working to make ends meet while you kept destroying my loved one? Did you enjoy it when I finally had to leave my job to care full time for my loved one because I feared for his safety?

Do you find it funny to watch my loved one struggle to find words or when he says the wrong words? Do you find it funny when I have to repeat myself over and over throughout the day because you have taken away his ability to remember?

I try really hard each day to be caring and patient. As you know, some days it is difficult and I do fail, but when I am successful, I hope that really upsets you. It makes me feel great when I am successful and gives me joy thinking my success upsets you.

It feels that you are fighting at every turn to make my life miserable. Just when I think I have things figured out, you decide to add a twist or a turn and I have to start all over again.

I am sure you have so many more tricks up your

sleeve and there is so much more to come, but I am ready for whatever you have to throw at us.

On behalf of my loved one, I will not stop fighting you and I will never let you feel welcomed. I am here for the long haul and no matter how difficult you make it for me or my loved one, I will still be here fighting to get you out of our home.

I do have to ask one more question. Why did you pick us? Why do you pick anyone? What exactly is your criteria?

There is so much more I would like to say to you, but I consider myself a lady and I am sure you know how I feel about you.

I pray that someday soon, there will be a medical breakthrough and that you will no longer exist. It is my prayer that you will no longer be able to be an uninvited guest in anyone's home.

You are just evil!

A LONELY JOURNEY

Now that really felt good for me! Isn't your letter to dementia long overdue?

—Undefeated

DEMENTIA HAS TAUGHT ME

Patience! (I would love to capitalize this one, but I don't want to appear that I have run out of patience.)

I am stronger than I think.

I am a fighter!

I am not alone. Caregivers worldwide are dealing with this disease.

You find out who your real friends are.

You find out what family members really are thicker than water and those who are not.

Doctors are not always right.

It is important to advocate for your loved one.

Empathy for your loved one is important. You really need to wear their shoes to fully understand their day.

What works today may not work tomorrow. Today I was able to avert his negative thoughts with my humor, but tomorrow it may not work.

Support groups are priceless.

Good friends can make a bad day good. Sharing my feelings with a good friend is great therapy.

Taking deep breaths does really help especially when my patience are running out.

Don't stop researching the disease. There may be new medical information.

I am only human.

I cannot do this alone.

Getting enough sleep is important not only for him, but for myself as well. Adequate sleep helps my patience immensely.

Some people, who are uneducated about dementia, have a misconception that dementia is contagious. Dementia is NOT contagious.

A LONELY JOURNEY

God is my strength.

I am an awesome caring caregiver.

I could continue sharing, but I would say these are the highlights of what dementia has taught me.

—*Still Learning*

DIAGNOSIS PROCESS

I lost my mother to a mixed form of dementia. To be specific, a combination of Lewy Body and Alzheimer's Disease. She passed away just over 4 years ago, and it is an understatement to say she was an incredible mother. But she was! And she impacted my life in so many wonderful ways, so of course, I miss her every day, but she is still with me and that is such comfort to know.

The disease took her at 74 years young and the symptoms started for her in her early sixties...way too early for such a vibrant, healthy person with so much to live for—eight grandchildren, four daughters with four sons-in-law, and one adoring husband. Not to mention all the friends and other family members she indeed also positively impacted.

Yes, this disease is truly heartbreaking, because it robs us of our loved ones, and is so unrelenting. However, I believe, it can also empower us to do better, and that is why I am sharing my story—So this is for you, Mom!

To begin, the only reason I actually know what specific form of dementia my mother had was due to her insistence that we find out what actual form of dementia she had. Since an autopsy is currently the only way to confirm a diagnosis, that is what was done, but I will go into that later in my story.

At the beginning my mother's symptoms were varied—she tired easily, which was extremely unusual for her. Prior to the symptoms starting you would describe her as having an abundance of energy. She also had difficulty writing, reading, performing normal everyday tasks like tying her shoes or cooking, which she loved to do. Organizing things, which was one of her strengths also became difficult. For example, packing a suitcase was extremely frustrating and at this time she also experienced visual impairment. Her sense of distance and dimension were negatively impacted, and her eye doctor told her it was not her eyes but something else. Then there was an uncharacteristic emotional incident at Christmas when our entire family was gathered together. Where she became very angry and then paranoid while trying to teach the grandchildren a game. This was something a few years earlier she would have had no problem doing. Needless to say, it was scary to see this behavior from her.

After I returned home from the holidays, the incident gnawed at me. This prompted me to discuss it and other observations I had made with a few friends who advised me to have my Mom see a neurologist. I honestly hadn't thought of this.

A LONELY JOURNEY

Since her symptoms weren't necessarily memory loss, and she was so healthy in all other areas, the thought of Alzheimer's Disease was not on my radar. The possibility that it could be this was unnerving and hard to except, so I began reading any information I could find. (I understand now, that one of my coping mechanisms is equipping myself with knowledge.) I then talked to my parents about going to a neurologist.

First, I discussed it with my father who said if I talked to my mother and she was willing to go, he would go along with it. In this discussion he also shared things with me that had been happening that I was unaware of at the time. I realized, that I had opened the door to this new reality, and this was the first step. Acknowledging that something is changing in someone that you love, even if that is the last thing you want to acknowledge.

I talked to my mother next and she was actually

relieved that someone was acknowledging the change in her and wanted to find answers with her. Of course, she was scared too, but more relieved than scared, which lends credence to the saying it's easier to deal with what you know than what you don't know.

I wish I could say that we then saw a neurologist and my mother was diagnosed, but it wasn't that easy. My parents did not live near any of their four daughters, and they were residing in a different state from all of us. The closest daughter was a 9-hour drive from them and for me, and two of my sisters, they were a 3-hour flight and 1-hour drive away. But knowing that help was needed, doctor appointments were made, and turns were taken for one of us to be there with them at the appointments.

My mom had the usual battery of neuro-psych tests and then we met with a neurologist, who informed us that she did not have Alzheimer's disease and referred us to a rheumatologist. We had a brief sigh of relief until another doctor seeing her for pain referred her to a neurologist again. This time we scheduled the next neurologist visit near where two of us, daughters lived. We had high hopes, but again we received no diagnosis.

So, long story short—she saw 4 different neurologists, in 4 different cities and never received a definitive diagnosis. However, that is not the end of the story or the point of this.

The last neurologist did actually help us by explaining to us that dementia comes in many forms and likened it to the color blue and the large spectrum of colors that define blue. And that a person with dementia could fall anywhere on that dementia spectrum depending on so many individual factors. He advised us not to focus on what actual dementia inflicted Mom and that even though we could not define it what mattered most was what we did and how we cared for her. This may sound simple, but to a family who was focused on getting the answer—this was the answer! Our focus needed to be on caring for her, and this helped us plan, accept and concentrate on being the best caregivers for her.

I started taking caregiving courses, which lead my sister and father to do the same. And we were very fortunate to eventually move my mom and my dad near my sister and me who live in the same town. This allowed the benefits of them seeing more of the grandchildren and the sharing of caregiving, and per her wishes, we were able to keep her at home until the end. All this, I believe, would not have happened if our focus had not shifted from "what is it?" to "what can we do?" Because I truly believe there is so MUCH we CAN DO to make a difference as caregivers. My mom made it easy, because once we listened, we did what she taught us, but we all don't have amazing role models, but I know we all can learn. So, my advice to a fellow caregiver is: be open to learning—keep trying and ask yourself, "What can I do?"

As a side note: Knowing my Mother's wishes to have a definitive diagnosis, my husband and I enrolled in an Alzheimer's study at a University, where they except brain tissue for the study of the disease. We are in the clinical core study where they are charting someone with parental history (me) and someone without (him). We go in for a physical each year and have both donated our brain tissue upon death, which gave us the benefit of a definitive diagnosis for my Mom.

—Amy H. Molepske © 2018

GOD HAS MY BACK

I will admit my life as a caregiver is quite stressful. Each day is a challenge. I wish I were more perfect. I wish I could be more kind and gentle and patient and caring. I really do try, but I fail some days. Most days, thankfully, I am successful.

My religion has been a great source of comfort and strength in my role as a caregiver for my husband. I would like to think that my husband would do the same for me, if our roles were reversed.

I will admit that I feel really challenged some days, but I like to think that it only makes me stronger for the next time, or at the very least, I hope that I learn from the challenge. I like to think that there are special places in heaven for caregivers. At

A LONELY JOURNEY

least it is nice to think there is.

Yes, there are days that I think I cannot do this. Days that I feel that I cannot get through another day or another moment sometimes. But somehow, that seems to be when I seem to get my second wind and when I seem to feel God's presence the most. I know I cannot possibly do this alone, nor am I doing it alone.

I am thankful for my faith and for God as I would hate to think what my life would be like without either one. May God bless you all on your journey. I believe He travels with each and every one of us every moment of our day, even though we don't realize it and often times we forget He is there by our side.

—Blessings

HAVE YOU SEEN MY SPOUSE?

Where is my spouse? I know he is in that body somewhere unable to express himself to me. How do I reach him?

This has been the most difficult part for me. We used to laugh. We had an active social life. We enjoyed each other's company. We did so much together and we had plans for so much more to come.

I have found simple things such as music that he enjoys seems to calm him. He also seems to enjoy a soft massage on his arm, hands or upper and lower back. He has never liked the feel of lotion or oil on his skin for some reason, so I do not use lotions or oils.

Food has become very important to him and lots

of it. I have been told it may be his mind does not recall that he has eaten and he wants to eat again. I try to give him snacks in small pieces in hopes that the motion of taking the small pieces will shorten the length of time that he wants to eat. Does that make sense? As some caregivers say, "Whatever works."

Another strange thing about food is his taste buds seemed to have changed. Foods he would never have eaten before suddenly seem to be his favorites? That certainly surprised me.

Not long after he was diagnosed, when we dined out, he started ordering two entrees. Naturally, he only ate one and the other would be packed up to go home. After that, I started to order for him, but that seemed to upset him so we stopped dining out. I was told this had something to do with his inability to make decisions.

I wish I had some prolific advice to share, but

for right now I feel like I am right in the middle of the forest just wondering what tomorrow will bring.

I think we may be nearing the end of our journey. So at this stage I am going to do "whatever works" to make the journey easier on us both.

—Anonymous

*Ever wonder how you can
help a caregiver?*

HOW CAN YOU HELP ME?

As a caregiver for my husband, my day is consumed with assisting TJ with his daily needs and, of course, periodic medical appointments. Although, I really do enjoy caring for TJ most days I have to admit I am exhausted and dream of the having the luxury to sleep in or maybe a relaxing bubble bath.

TJ is the love of my life. God willing, I plan to care for him until "death us do part." In no way do I mean for any of this to sound like I am complaining as I do enjoy caring for my husband.

Answering the question, "How can I help?" is difficult, but over the years I have come up with a few answers.

How can you help? Basically, the biggest help you can give is to help the caregiver themselves as caring for their loved ones is personal. As his caregiver, I am familiar with his routine, his wants and needs. I know my husband would not like someone else assisting with his shower or other hygiene needs and so I respect that on his behalf.

How can you help? Your understanding would be at the top of my list. Understanding why I am not the same friend, mom or sister I used to be. I highly value our relationship, but understand that I can no longer be spontaneous as I have to arrange for someone to be with TJ.

If I am not able to accept your invitation, please understand and please keep trying for another day. Our relationship is precious to me, but my life has changed. And if I have to cancel, even last minute, please understand.

How can you help? Support me. Listen. Especially when I am feeling down. Even if I have shared similar stories before.

HOW CAN YOU HELP ME

How can you help? Let me know the care I provide is appreciated. Thank me for taking care of your father, brother, sister, uncle, friend. Kind words won't cost you anything.

How can you help? Don't judge me. Don't tell me what I should be doing as this does not help me. I am doing the best I can. I am already reading everything I can get my hands on about dementia. I am already consulting with specialists. Unless you are in my shoes, you cannot possibly really know what I am going through.

How can you help? Don't tell me you feel my husband doesn't have dementia. You are not with him 24/7, so consider yourself fortunate he has not shown you that side of himself in the short time you have visited with him.

How can you help? Don't add guilt to my plate by asking me to do favors for you. As much as I would like to, there unfortunately, is no room in my day and I feel bad when I have to tell you no.

How can you help? I would love to have coffee with you at my kitchen table. Please call ahead.

How can you help? Make me laugh! Tell me about interesting things going on in your life. I don't get much outside interaction, as a caregiver, so conversation is a luxury for me.

How can you help? A simple smile, a hug, kind words, a small gesture means so much.

In summary, just realize I dearly need your support, unconditional love and understanding to help me to be a good caregiver and I need lots and lots of hugs!

—Shared with Love

HOW FAR I HAVE JOURNEYED

When I look back I can't believe how far our journey has already taken us. I remember:

The days of desperately seeking a diagnosis for my husband that made sense.

That sinking feeling, the punch in the gut, when the doctors finally find a diagnosis and give you the news even though you somewhat expected it.

That lonely feeling not knowing what to do next.

That deer in the headlight feeling.

My whole body and mind feeling numb to the news.

That inner doubting if my love is strong enough even though I knew it was.

The reaction from our children.

The reaction from my family.

The reaction of denial from his family.

The reaction of friends with a mixture of support, denial and detachment.

The reaction of co-workers.

Finding ways to keep him engaged with life.

The reaction of employers.

Trial and error with medications.

Numerous medical appointments.

Finding a new place to live.

Finding ways to motivate him.

Finding ways to keep him engaged with life. inding ways to keep his spirits up and mine.

Finding ways to be with friends as a couple.

Finding support groups for me to attend so I am not isolated entirely.

Finding ways to keep him engaged with life. Finding ways to keep his spirits up and mine.

Finding ways to take care of myself.

Selling our house to downsize as I did not have the ability or time to take on the responsibilities of being a homeowner myself. Selling our home full of memories. The home where we raised our children.

Now that I feel I have found what still makes him happy, I concentrate on those things. When I have a chance I get out and do something that makes me happy, even if it is lunch by myself.

I enjoy learning from other caregivers through reading books, such as this one, dementia related Facebook pages and websites. I do find a lot of useful advice from other caregivers. I am also interested, of course, in what the latest research findings are.

If you are just in the beginning of your journey, my advice is don't despair. You are not alone. You can do this. You are strong.

—*Be Strong*

*Laughter is truly
good medicine*

HUMOR IS IMPORTANT

I cannot say enough about how important humor is in the life of a caregiver. Laughter has many times kept me from crying and has raised my spirits up.

I have found that laughter helps my husband as well, especially when he wants to dwell on something negative. I try to crack a joke about it and I can usually get a smile or laugh out of him probably because my attempt at a joke is usually pretty corny.

I was lucky to find the importance of laughter early on. I think I found it early, mostly because I was trying so hard to be strong for him and trying to keep my spirits up, as well, and trying not to cry and not to become depressed.

I will turn sitcoms on TV for us to watch as it is

much easier for him to watch a 30 minute program as opposed to a movie. He can get through a movie, but tends to need several breaks, so a movie takes us a bit longer to watch than normal.

We have grandchildren who love to come visit grandpa. They always bring a smile to his face. They are in what I call "the fun years" where they are still discovering the world and it is still so exciting to them. Like any grandparent, I think I could write a book about all the funny things that come out of their mouths. At least humorous to us.

My husband doesn't like me reading to him. I am not sure how well he is still reading himself. It seems to me that he is quite a bit slower at reading and probably comprehending less than he used to be. I recently experienced this when we were sharing some reading material. He was getting quite annoyed with me turning the pages before he was finished. I remember him being a faster reader than I was.

I consider myself fortunate that my husband still has his sense of humor. I have heard from other caregivers that is not always the case and they are dealing with anger from their loved ones towards them. I do have to admit some days his humor is a bit corky, but it sure beats the opposite.

In general, he is pretty cordial in public and at family gatherings. I do see that he tires more easily, which I suppose is from the extra stimulating surroundings. I am careful to not stay longer than he can tolerate.

I do fear that I am hiding behind all this humor and that someday I will finally have to face all the emotions I have been hiding behind with my use of humor. Until that day comes, I am choosing to laugh because it seems to make him happy.

—Smile

Sleep is precious

I AM TIRED

I am so tired. I never thought I would be or could be so tired. Caregiving takes a lot out of you no matter how much you love someone.

I have had tests for physical reasons such as thyroid, vitamin D deficiency, you name it, but I think I probably have the other D word—depression. Nothing seems to help.

It is very depressing work to be a 24/7 caregiver for a loved one. It is very thankless work. It seems everyone including books and television are always telling you how you could do better instead of telling you what a great job you are doing and that you are appreciated.

I am not expecting a banner or parade, but just a smile and a genuine pat on the back would help instead of suggestions of what I should try when they have never been in my shoes or in the shoes of any caregiver. I know my husband, in his present state, would never think to thank me. As a rule, he wasn't the most thankful person before, but I think we had our unspoken ways.

It is hard to care for someone and yet you have to do everything yourself. He used to be our fix it guy and now I have to do the best I can or if I can't fix it, then I have to call someone or a professional to help out. I can't ask him for help with the laundry, cleaning, dishwashing, putting groceries away, washing floors or even running to the store for errands. There is still twice the amount of work, but only one worker now. We don't qualify for any assistance, yet just scraping by.

So I do my best. Some days the dishes have to wait until tomorrow. Some weeks, the floors don't get washed. We manage. I just have to lower my standards a bit. I admit that is difficult for me to do, but for now I can only do what my energy level allows me to do.

I never understood the life of a 24/7 caregiver before, but I definitely do now. Caregivers are amazing, resilient, loving, patient, hardworking, humble, kind, selfless angels here on earth!

—Anonymous

Counting Blessings

I FEEL BLESSED

Okay, so there are days that I do feel down, but in general I feel blessed. My life isn't always what I expected or wanted it to be but I choose to count my blessings and hope I can continue to do so on my life's journey.

I can still communicate with my husband so we can still laugh together. He doesn't laugh too much anymore, but I find victory in just getting him to smile.

We can still do a bit of traveling. We actually can do a lot of the things that we used to do just that I learned that I have to modify things a bit.

If and when we do something is based on how he feels that day. If he is agitated it is definitely a stay home day. If he is having a good day, then we make plans to get out of the house. It may be just to get groceries, but getting out of the house is good for us both.

For larger family gatherings, I try to arrive early when there are fewer people there and when I see him becoming overwhelmed, then I know it is time to leave. He usually will nap when we get home as the extra stimulation tires him. I do find smaller groups work best for him.

For me right now, I see caregivers in all sorts of situations that are dealing with far worse than I am so that is why I do count my blessings. My heart truly goes out to those of you who are in the harder stages of caregiving. I know this will change for me in the future, possibly near future, but for now I am counting my blessings.

—Blessed

I HIGHLY RECOMMEND THIS

I have to confess this is actually my second submission for this book. Even if neither of my submissions are accepted for the book, I know I will still feel whole as a result of submitting my journey.

I sent this second submission because I want to share that I found the relief, therapy or whatever you want to call it was tremendous. I was amazed. Just putting my feelings down on paper and sharing my feelings was amazingly therapeutic. I think actually sharing was the most therapeutic part because I was actually putting my feelings out for others. Just writing my feelings on paper felt like I was still keeping it to myself.

I, wholeheartedly, recommend to anyone that is reading this book to put your thoughts on paper and share them with someone. I had no idea sharing my journey would result in such relief for myself. I didn't realize how much I was keeping inside and not releasing and perhaps not even allowing myself to feel.

The tension I carried between my shoulder blades has seriously diminished. I never would have expected such a change. I am not saying this could be true for everyone, but I do know that it has changed my attitude in so many ways.

If you ever have an opportunity to take part in a project like this I highly recommend you do so. It's priceless and you are helping others as well.

By documenting and submitting my journey, I found it forced me to face my feelings. Feelings I had unknowingly suppressed. I was so busy taking care of my husband and worrying about how he felt that I wasn't taking care of my own emotions.

I appreciated this opportunity! Again, to

I HIGHLY RECOMMEND THIS

anyone reading this, I strongly recommend writing your journey today–even if you don't share it with anyone, but the real benefit comes with sharing.

—*Anonymous*

A LONELY JOURNEY

The diagnosis can be like
"a punch in the stomach"

JOHN

It's been almost two years since John was diagnosed with dementia. "Probably of the Alzheimers type," she said. It's like a punch in the stomach even though you knew it all along. Since then I've read about as much as I care to on the subject and life has certainly changed for us. One thing for certain, most of the changes have had to come from me. My daily mantra is to be kind, patient and understanding. The path John is going down can't be fixed, I'm the one who must make changes. He is not the same person I've known for almost 47 years and sometimes I must remind myself of that.

I'd be lying if I said we had a wonderful, happy marriage. However, we did not fight. That is to say we did not yell, scream, swear or throw things at one another. We were much better at the silent treatment and that could go on for days, if necessary.

That all changed about 6 - 7 years ago when for very little reason John would be in my face yelling at the top of his lungs about something I may have implied or said in a way in which he did not like. This was new to me and besides feeling hurt and angry, I began wondering what brought that behavior on. Was it "Grumpy Old Man" syndrome? Gosh, he wasn't that old. Then another thing starting happening that made me wonder if there wasn't something else going on. His driving. He seemed to point the car in whatever direction and just drive. It was almost as if he were in a trance. He seldom used the signal lights, made quick turns without warning and drove down the state highway at dangerously slow speeds. At one point I told him his driving scared me and I would do the driving. I did take over driving which calmed my nerves.

Getting John evaluated took some persistence on my part. After all, he did not look like someone with dementia. He certainly looked years younger than his age, 69, at the time. He was physically fit, not overweight and very active. He taught for many years so he kept his mind sharp by researching and preparing lessons. I don't think I was taken seriously because of his physical state. After accompanying John to several of his appointments, his family doctor suggested he was depressed and once that was addressed he'd be his old self. I couldn't argue with the depression theory. However, this did not help with the cognitive concerns I had been watching decline over the past two to three years.

Neuropsychological testing was a long grueling five hours for both of us. Leaving us in a state of numbness. Overcome by sadness and bewilderment....what now?

We have always heated our home with wood. We love the warmth and watching the crackling fire in the woodstove over a glass of wine. Besides, John loved being in the woods, cutting and clearing wind falls and dead trees. This past winter, after being fully retired, I joined in the hauling and throwing of wood into the basement. We decided I would fill the cart, push it to the basement, throw it in through the open window and John would stack it. I pushed my first cart full, threw it down and headed back to the woodshed for another load. By the time I got back John had thrown the first load back out the window. This was going to be a long day!

So I decided we would both work outside and push the cart to the open window and stack it together when we were done. As fast as I could load the cart, John would unload it and put it back on the woodpile. After enough coaching he got it right!

John is also obsessed with his wallet. He wants it on him at all times. I suppose it's a hold on his identity. Problem is he keeps hiding it. After searching, sometimes for hours on end, he'll ask, "Well, how did it get there?" I've found it under the waste basket, inside a book, under the bed, high up on a shelf, under a pile of towels, the list of places goes on and on.

Our son-in-law suggested a wallet locator. Perfect! I searched the internet and found one I thought might work. A small plastic disk which would be inserted into the wallet and an app would be downloaded onto my cell phone. When the wallet was missing I could use my phone to locate it. I explained as best I could what the little plastic disk was for and how we wouldn't be spending so much time looking for the "misplaced" wallet.

A LONELY JOURNEY

As expected he couldn't find his wallet one evening. "No problem," I said, "Let me get my phone and we will locate your wallet." Beep, beep, beep...I followed the beeping sound to our den. We keep a 4 foot Alpine tree standing on a wooden chest up for most of the winter. The beeping was coming from the tree. Did he put the wallet in the tree? But I couldn't find it anywhere. Yet the beeping continued.

Being frustrated and annoyed at not being able to find the wallet I called off the search for the night and said we'd pick up the trail first thing in the morning. Which is what we did. I kept following the beep and finally picked up the tree and fabric under it and there was the wallet finder. He had hid it under the tree! Great we found the locator, but not the wallet. "John, the plastic disk must stay in the wallet to work." I honestly don't remember where we found the wallet that time.

JOHN

Presently, the wallet is missing. The urgency to find it has subsided somewhat. He still gets very upset and declares he has nothing, no money, nothing, because he doesn't have his wallet. (I did wise-up some time ago and removed his driver's license, insurance card and health information and put it in an old wallet which I keep in my purse.)

John has always been an outdoor person. He has grown to hate the cold, but does like to go outside. This past winter when he would venture out to shovel the sidewalk or work in the wood shed, he would layer one stocking cap on top of the other. Seeing him walk around with three stocking caps perched on top of his head was quite a sight and all I could think of was the children's book, "*Caps for Sale.*" I often wonder what the UPS man thought when he saw him outside with a variety of stocking caps piled on his head!

He has also become obsessed with pieces of

wood and bark which he spends hours on coloring or painting, then mounting on a base. Every room in the house has a collection of his artwork. There are boxes full and some are hanging from strings in the windows. He also gives them away to friends and feels very proud doing it. This is one of the areas where I've had to adapt. I compliment him on his "works of art," but have to walk away from the messes he leaves behind chipping away at the wood or adding glitter paint to everything. I cannot take the joy he finds in creating these "masterpieces" away from him. Who knows, maybe one day his art will be on display at an exhibition somewhere! (I have to admit though, sometimes when I'm in need of a piece of kindling wood I look over the collection and carefully remove one or two pieces that would help get that fire started.)

I don't know where we are headed from day to day, but after almost 47 years of marriage I know that the glue that has held us together and will keep us in this partnership is our common bond to our home and property, our love of our family and friends, and our commitment to the institution of marriage…for better or for worse!

—Rose

Life Changes

LONG LONG JOURNEY

Part 1 Lost and Lonesome

Written September 2016

I have always felt that I've had a charmed and blessed life — a beautiful and loving wife of 46 years, five caring and supportive children, and a thirty year challenging and fulfilling career as a nurse. I always told people that, even after years of marriage, my wife Doris, and I were still celebrating our honeymoon.

In 2004, Doris began to notice that she felt confused. In 2006 I retired because I could tell that she was going to need help. For 25 years we had enjoyed traveling around the U.S. So when I retired I thought now we would have time to travel. I had always enjoyed woodworking and building things. I thought now I would have time to do something entirely different from my career. I told everyone that I was going to "pound nails" with Habitat for Humanity.

None of that worked out. Having a spouse with dementia is a whole new ball game, a 24 hour/7 day a week responsibility. We limped along from year to year with new challenges and different behaviors each year. I was lost and lonesome.

As she became more paranoid and anxious, Doris didn't want to visit people. We'd drive to Milwaukee or to Minneapolis to visit one of the kids and as we drove into the driveway she'd suddenly insist, "I don't want to be here. I want to go home." We'd just arrive for a family get together or a wedding and she'd say, "We gotta go." We'd go out to eat at a restaurant with the kids for Mother's Day and she'd refuse to eat and wander around the restaurant or into the kitchen. When

I'd hug my daughter or granddaughter goodbye, she'd start pounding on my arm because I was making out with this strange woman. All of this was emotionally frustrating for both of us and for the kids.

When the phone rings, she says "I don't want company." When the kids call, she will frequently refuse to talk to them. We've tried medication but that only made the anxiety, the delusions, and the anger even worse.

On the other hand, the paradox of this disease is that for years now she's looking for the kids, especially at bed time—but not the kids as adults but as teenagers. She won't go to bed, roams the house, full of questions: "Where are the kids? Where did they say they were going?" She opens up all the beds and makes up the couches with blankets for sleeping, leaves the front door unlocked because "the kids are coming."

A LONELY JOURNEY

Lately she has periods when she doesn't recognize me. "Who are you? What's your wife's name? It can't be Doris. I'm the only Doris I know."

There are certainly times when she's her old self—loving and laughing, philosophizing about something I don't remember. Lately she's reminiscing about her grade school days at St. Therese. We wash dishes together three times a day because that seems to be when she likes to talk about her family and my family. My beautiful and loving wife is still in there. It's just that a brain fog makes it hard for her to be herself.

This past winter our daughter gave her a therapy doll for her birthday. When she opened the box, she fell in love with it and takes the baby everywhere, along to church, walking the mall pushing a stroller, sleeping on the pillow next to her. It has relieved some of the anxiety and has been a topic for socializing with people we meet.

About a year and a half ago we visited the Thompson Community Center for lunch and discovered the Fox Valley Memory Project Resource Center. On the spur of the moment we joined the choir called "On a Positive Note," a choir for people with memory loss and their care partners. We have both come to enjoy singing together. The Fox Valley Memory Project has gotten free tickets for dress rehearsals and we've attended musicals at UW Fox Valley and Xavier High School. We also attend some of the Memory Cafés, especially those involving music.

I have really felt the social isolation of this disease. What has helped me personally has been the monthly support group for caregivers. When I found that group, I found the help I'd been looking for. I found other caregivers going through the same struggles I was having. It surprised me how similar the symptoms of dementia are from person to person. My next step will be to explore the respite care that I know I'm going to need.

So, the Fox Valley Memory Project has helped me as far as socializing for Doris, as far as the two of us singing together, and as far as me finding the support I need to continue this long journey.

In our kitchen we have Holly Hobbie plates decorating the soffit. Every morning I look at the plate over the sink that reads: "Happiness is having someone to care for." So I believe my life is still blest.

Part 2 Decisions and Frustration

Written February 2017

I have worked in Long Term Care as a nurse for over 30 years, but even from that side of the coin, we always said that institutional living was a last resort. Everyone preferred to live in his or her own home as long as possible. However, there came a point when it was no longer possible for the family.

Now that I am on the other side of the coin —a caregiver for a spouse with dementia—it is a whole different ballgame—a 24 hour 7 day a week responsibility, a responsibility that sometimes becomes heavy.

There are days that my wife's paranoia and anxiety make her so angry that I wonder how long I can do this. I wonder if this is the best situation for her or for me and my health.

But then there are days when she is sweet and gracious and social, philosophizing about something I don't understand, free flowing association of ideas about days past when she was 5 years old or 12 years old. These are days when I say that this isn't so bad. In fact, she's a glimmer of her old self.

The fluctuation between these two extremes occurs from day to day, sometimes from hour to hour or even oftener.

And I vacillate. Is keeping her home best for her or me? I think she might do well in an institution. But then she might have a catastrophic reaction to being forced out of her home and into a facility. I've seen that reaction in the feelings some residents have for what they perceive that their families have done to them.

And then I think of the changes in my lifestyle, how I might get involved with volunteer work, like Habitat for Humanity. But then I think of being alone in this house. I've never lived alone and I don't know how I would do it. Then I think that at least for now we have some level of companionship. It's better than being alone.

And I think about the changes that have occurred over the past 12 years that she's had this disease. Some things have improved. She no longer has a catastrophic reaction when I leave a tip at a restaurant. She no longer leaves the front door unlocked throughout the night because "the kids are coming home." So perhaps some of today's behaviors will fade over the next year.

And so the vacillation goes back and forth. I now have her Power of Attorney activated, so the burden of the decision rests on my shoulders. Either option of living arrangements is going to have its burdens. I would like to keep her home as long as possible, because this is our home of 40 years. I've heard testimony of people who've kept a loved one in the home to the end and advocate doing that. But everybody's situation is different. We can each only do the best we can.

Whether my wife stays at home or were to go to an institution, she's leaving me gradually, going away ever so slowly. I would just like to make her days as happy and enjoyable as it is possible with this disease. I think the deciding factor will be if I can handle the behavioral dimensions and if my health holds up. Someone once said, "You'll know when you can't do it anymore."

Part 3 Kindness and Survival

Written February 2018

It is now thirteen years since Doris was diagnosed with "Memory Loss". During the year before that she noticed that she felt confused. The kids say that they noticed signs even before that. But it was after open heart surgery in 2005 that the memory loss became evident.

Doris' physical health has been relatively stable. In the past year she has refused to take her cholesterol or blood pressure medications. Except for her thyroid pills her doctor has discontinued her medications and discontinued monitoring lab work.

Doris' behavior has gone through a roller coaster of symptoms. Presently she doesn't recognize me or our children, or at times, her own name. Only occasionally can she verbalize the names of her five children. She'll even say, "I didn't marry anyone." Although she seldom recognizes me as her husband, she is very dependent on me and sees me as her caregiver or her driver. It stings when she asks, "Where's John?" If I try to tell her that I'm John, it only causes a puzzled look of concern and confusion. Instead I say, "He's at work" and she seems satisfied with that.

She sleeps an average of fourteen hours a day, but she is now losing her sense of day and night, frequently up, turning on all the lights, and ready "to go" for a couple hours in the middle of the night. She will not be convinced that it's night time. She insists we need to "go to church." Sometimes feeding her or going for a car ride can help.

In fact, her routine is to eat a meal and hurriedly wash the dishes, because "we have to get going to church." We drive a mile to the Fox River Mall and walk once around. We do this once, twice, sometimes three times in a day. She pushes a stroller with her baby doll. The stroller also provides support so that she doesn't fall. Most of the merchants are very friendly and know us by sight.

She seems driven to "go" all the time, but doesn't know where she wants to go or what she wants to do. She wants to go out to eat regularly, but roams around the restaurant trying to find a satisfactory booth or table at which she is willing to sit. She doesn't want to be near anyone else. She can't make a decision about what to eat or even choose between beef and chicken. If we go out with family, she refuses to sit with them but takes a separate booth, sometimes even walking out of the restaurant. Even at home, if any of the kids come over for a meal, she'll refuse to come to the table.

With her disinhibition and mood swings she can become belligerent, swearing, raising her fist, even striking out. I think she sees herself with all these "strangers" and that stresses her to the breaking point.

The natural stubbornness that she has is compounded by stress, especially in social situations. When we arrive for a visit at the house of one of the kids, she'll refuse to get out of the car, or if she does get out, will ask to go home in a matter of minutes. At Memory Cafes she will refuse to get out of the car and we frequently just drive back home. She loves music but getting her into the venue for music is a struggle. She's been part of the choir "On a Positive Note," but at performances refuses to sit with the choir. She's trying to exercise some level of control in her life. I used to envy those caregivers with a spouse who was docile and came along calmly to any event, or who liked to sit at home and watch TV or spend time with hobbies or activities. But I shouldn't have been surprised that she was not like that, because Doris was always dominant and stubborn and wanted her own way.

Like a toddler she doesn't know how to deal with her stress, sometimes acting out physically, stomping her feet on the car dash or repeatedly banging the car door into the garage wall. She gets upset when she sees me reading. She snatches the newspaper and crumples it up. At times she says things that cut to the quick like, "You used to be a nice guy. What happened to you?" This can even escalate to a catastrophic reaction, where she leaves the house, walks away and says, "I'll call the police." It seems that her stress builds until she has to act on it. The only solution I've found is to give her my full attention and do whatever she wants. It's hard.

When one of our daughters or my sister comes

for a visit and I talk to them, Doris can become very angry. Probably because she cannot follow the conversation or because she's not the center of the conversation. Because of her disinhibition, she blurts out her anger, usually at me, "What are you trying to do? I don't like what you're doing. You're an ass" and other vulgarities. When this happens between the two of us, I've learned not to let that bother me. But when it happens in front of others, it does bother me to the point that my stomach feels tied in knots and I can't sleep at night. That's what I call stress. I'm angry when it happens, but I can't say anything in retaliation. So it festers inside and I don't know how to deal with it.

Sometimes I think she'd have less stress if we stayed away from memory cafes and family get togethers. I've been unable to get her interested in activities like puzzles, coloring or games. Occasionally she has strung cheerios for the birds.

Occasionally she lets me read her a story. She likes looking at photo albums.

Now when we're at home she's getting to the point of saying, "I want to go home. This is not my home. Take me home. My mother told me to come home." I wonder would she be more comfortable living in a nursing home? I believe she would experience the same anxiety to "go home."

On the other hand, she can have such a sweet personality. When she's feeling good and her stomach is full, she can talk one-on-one for forty-five minutes in a kind of verbal casserole, jumbling together all kinds of things from her memory and from who knows where, confabulating a story, occasionally blending in what she sees before her eyes, philosophizing about life and people and her role in the cosmos. That's why I fell in love with her. Of course, now it's all incomprehensible stories, a monologue with very little cohesion.

She's having more and more difficulty with word finding, using the correct word, or even understanding words spoken to her. She loves when people make a fuss over her "baby" but becomes argumentative if someone says, "Oh, it's just a doll." She also loves to tell people about her musical family.

Lately, when I tuck her into bed and kiss her good night and tell her that I love her, she'll usually say, "I love you too" or "Thank you very much for helping me. I love you so much." And with a twinkle in her eye she'll sometimes say, "We have to be careful."

Before bed I do some exercises and deep breathing meditation, but there are still nights when I lie awake in the middle of the night, my mind too busy to slow down. Doris dislikes TV, but likes to listen to music videos of the 1950's and 1960's folk music. After hearing this music repeatedly the words of the songs go through my head at night over and over.

I feel that my partner of 48 years is going away. And I wonder about my wife "How fearful and anxious you are as you try to make sense of this fading world."

I cope through a number of strategies. I try to get to the YMCA twice a week for flexibility and strength training with Silver Sneakers. This also provides some camaraderie. I walk the treadmill in the basement thirty minutes three times a week, while using the time to pray my unique form of the rosary. I also find stress relief through journaling the struggles and the good times. After putting my thoughts on paper, I can let go and go to sleep.

I enjoy reading. I've joined the book discussion group called The Mug Club to delve into some very good books. The ones that have spoken most significantly to my situation include:

Learning to Speak Alzheimer's

Keeping Love Alive as Memories Fade

Creating Moments of Joy

My Two Elaines

Books, along with support groups I've joined, have been life savers. In order to attend these, I've been able to hire very competent respite care. I read and go to all these things for continued motivation, because it takes a lot of motivation to try to create moments of joy and to survive this life with kindness.

There are so many things I'd like to do: read, watch the news or political commentary on TV, cut up a fallen tree in the back yard, or varnish the bathroom woodwork. But it's difficult to get done even the essentials: cutting the grass, shoveling the snow, shopping for groceries, cleaning the house, fixing a leaking toilet. I need to do these when she's sleeping.

Because Doris usually sleeps until ten or eleven in the morning, I have a couple hours for "my time" doing chores around the house or reading. But once she is awake, she wants my time to be her time. She wants my full attention. She wants what she wants and right now. She can have a catastrophic reaction if I'm working on a repair project or cutting the lawn. So my full time job right now is caring for my wife. One day is so much like the next that I sometimes can't recall what we've done and wonder if I'm losing my memory and my mind.

In hindsight, I wish we had faced the diagnosis years ago and got comfortable with the word "Alzheimer's," Doris has never admitted that she has any problem, other than occasionally saying she feels confused. Now it is too late because she has very little insight.

Another prayer I use while on the treadmill is the Prayer of St. Francis:

Make me a channel of your peace.

Where there is hatred, let me bring your love.

Where there is injury, your pardon, Lord,

and where there's doubt, true faith in you.

Make me a channel of your peace.

Where there's despair in life, let me bring hope.

Where there is darkness, only light,

and where there's sadness, ever joy.

Oh, Master, grant that I may never seek so much

to be consoled as to console,

To be understood as to understand,

to be loved as to love with all my soul.

Make me a channel of your peace.

It is in pardoning that we are pardoned.

In giving of ourselves that we receive,

and in dying that we're born to eternal life.

In the times of darkness and sadness and anger
when she lashes out with the words, "I hate you."
I need to be the one to bring her some light and love

and moments of joy. In the times when I long for compassion and understanding and love from my partner, I remember that it is more blessed to give than to receive. I try to give my all to this one-sided relationship. It's hard.

My prayer is that I live as long as she does, that I will be able to bring her what moments of joy that I can, and in the catastrophic moments to just hang on and survive.

—John Weyers @ 2018

LOSING JOHN

Nothing ever stays the same and change is usually difficult—a lesson most of us eventually learn in life. Yet when we marry for better or worse, we don't really foresee the very essence of our relationships changing. But with Alzheimer's disease it does, and it is a slow heartbreaker.

Six years ago this past October, my husband John was worried that his memory was slipping and talked to his doctor about it. This then led to a series of psychological mental tests and an MRI, and culminated with a diagnosis of "Mild Cognitive Impairment." I remember us sitting in the car afterward trying to digest this, and even yet in my mind's eye, can still see the leaves spinning around the parking lot in mini tornadoes as we talked.

A LONELY JOURNEY

My husband was sad on my behalf and went right to trying to problem solve what was going to happen to me without him. I, on the other hand, was disbelieving, feeling that he probably just wasn't willing to let go of even an ounce of his mental acuity to normal aging without overreacting.

As I write this, we have been married 45 years and John is eight years older than me. My attraction to him began with his humor, his gentleness, his willingness to talk about feelings for hours on end, his faith in God, and his ardent desire to please and serve others. He was fun, spontaneous, a little disorganized, but creative. He made me laugh.

In spite of his progression to a "probable" Alzheimer's diagnosis three years ago, and now a "firm" diagnosis based on behavioral and cognititive symptoms, he is still that same man.

It is my feelings that have changed. I have learned that love is not as much a feeling as a verb.

I have chosen to love him. The man I passionately longed to be alone with is more and more just the man I please and serve.

I miss the romance and my mind returns to the past, including old flames, with sadness. Even John's humor, where it all began, rarely catches me off guard enough to give me the spark I need and him the genuine response he desires.

It is difficult for us to talk to each other about anything now. This is where I miss him most. He can speak concrete, short and familiar phrases most the time, such as "look at the sky" or "want more coffee?" But he cannot think of the words he needs to convey, for example, what he is looking for. He is rarely able to express his feelings or reasons to me. I need to read his hand gestures and his moods to guess what he is trying to say. When I say something concretely simple such as, "She sure looks like Mother," he will only understand if it is repeated. But if I try to talk about an abstract idea or an analogical reason for something, he cannot follow.

His reasoning leads to misinterpretations of situations, even bordering on paranoia. I am alone with major medical and financial decisions. I am alone with getting our affairs in order. And I am alone with how I feel about things, but it occurs to me that he too probably feels just as alone in the same room with me, trapped within his mind.

Another sad aspect to this lack of communication is the loss of other friendships and entertaining. We have a handful of old friends who still travel to see us once in a while, but as for making new friends since our move to this town two years ago…what's the use of trying. John cannot talk to them so we do not inflict them with invitations.

His disorganization has augmented to an issue we deal with on a daily basis. Where are the keys, the glasses, the shoes, the hearing aids? Even though I organize and re-organize his drawers, a few days later, there are socks, t-shirts, sweaters and underwear in every drawer. His idea of organization is another flat surface or plastic bag. He does not want to get rid of anything except perhaps to another bag or bin in the garage. This lack of order is chaotic for me as a perfectionist in a small apartment.

One day, recently, our car horn kept making random "toots" in the garage. Since this garage is under someone else's apartment, we were both frantically looking for his keys. It turns out they were inside his shoe and nearly every step he took was setting off the horn! This lack of awareness is a reflection of his disorder.

The date, the year, the day of the week and "what is going on today" constantly slip his mind. Even though we have a large calendar in the kitchen with past days crossed off and the events of the day listed, he reads it, but asks me several times what we are doing.

Today, for instance, he sees that the calendar says "Caregiver Support Group" and he has asked three times if he is going. I tell him it is just for me. Then he turns around and asks me when he should be ready. I ask him, "For what?" He says, "The dentist." (I suppose this is because he heard me talking with the dentist office yesterday to confirm our appointments three weeks from now!)

He frequently asks me how old he is and how I figure that out. One day he asked me what year it was and I told him 2017. A half hour later he came to me with a large bag of canned goods to "give to the dog place by where we walk and turn left." Why? Because they were "too old," he said. They all expired in 2018 and 2019! He has little slips of paper all around the house with our address written on them. He is trying so hard, yet he cannot tell me what it is. Our phone number is out of the question!

As for fun and spontaneity, I am the poor creator of this in our family now. Ever the practical planner, the best I can come up with is, "Want to go to the thrift store with me?" You can imagine where that goes!

After a near traffic mishap, he voluntarily gave up driving a year and a half ago, so he no longer takes me on day trips or suggests romantic weekends. I could suggest something that might be affordable, but it would be a tense vs. scenic drive there and he would struggle with acclimating. Familiarity has become a comfort to him. The last place we went, he fell out of bed.

His faith is strong, but he is depressed, losing weight and frequently cries. He has not been able to tolerate antidepressants or Alzheimer's medication.

He focuses on the waning of this world and just wants Jesus to return and rescue us. He is happy to see his disease progress because he wants his life and our suffering to end soon. Whereas I still have some hopes in the future, he has none but this.

He loves when I read the Bible and pray with him. I have come to realize that I have the God-given task of his happiness and well-being and have been entrusted with his care just as if he were my child. By faith, I trust that God will never leave me nor forsake me, yet I must take some responsibility in this journey.

And also, as if he were my child, I spend much time explaining and re-explaining things. Whereas children eventually learn, John keeps losing the ground we covered. Little tasks he could handle he suddenly can't. Today, after two years of opening the garage door, he was searching around the garage for the button.

He is losing the ability to handle the TV remotes to find something he wants to watch. Twice this week, he put dirty dishes on top of clean dishes in the dishwasher. Maybe because he does something right much of the time, it is so difficult for me as a caregiver to remember that the general "progression" of the disease is backward — and that he isn't just trying to annoy me. I pray for patience every day.

My most valuable take away from Caregiver Support is that he may not remember what I said or did, but he will remember how I made him feel.

This is not the end of his story or my story. It may be closer to the beginning than the end and that worries me some—financially, physically and spiritually—I have a lot of growing up ahead of me! You may pass me walking down the street and not recognize me. I look older now and I am lonely.

True to my characteristic needs and the

openness of our relationship through the years, I asked my husband if he cared to hear this and cautiously shared it with him, explaining that his name had been changed for anonymity. There were no surprises for him and he teared up, which wasn't a surprise either. Then I hugged him, said "I love you, _____!" and kissed him hard and long on the lips. He quickly broke the corners of his kiss into a smile and quipped, "Just call me John!" We both ended up laughing, and oh, it felt so good!

—*Still Looking for John*

MEMORIES OF MOM

Being the oldest of eleven children, I have many wonderful memories of my Mom. We were raised on a farm in a small community. Years ago, you stayed at home and raised your children. You didn't work outside the home unless you were single. If you did work outside the home, usually the work would be housekeeping or midwife or teacher for example. In those days you could only be a teacher if you were single.

There was a lot of hard work and long hours living on the farm. When my parents got married, my grandfather bought a farm for my Dad that he had to pay back in installments. However, his Dad was killed in a farm accident when he fell from the beam in the barn onto machinery below. My Dad then had to pay back all his siblings over the years.

Meanwhile, my mother's mom was killed in a car accident the following year. This was so devastating for both my parents who were struggling with all the debt and hard work on the farm. They worked long hard hours.

They had horses then and eventually a tractor. Clothes were washed on a scrub board until they could afford a wringer washer. There were chickens, pigs, horses, cows, dogs and cats to feed, a big garden to tend, meals to make, and canning to be done for the winter. Hundreds of jars lined the shelves.

Mom also sewed almost all our clothes. There were six girls before they finally had two boys, then another two girls and then one more boy.

My parents worked very hard over the years to raise their large family. Eventually my brother took over the farm and they moved to a home nearby, but Dad stayed involved in helping on the farm. Mom still had a fairly big garden and still did some canning.

Mom was also involved in the ladies aid at church. She loved to crochet and knit as a pastime. She crocheted angels that they still use to decorate the Christmas tree at the church she used to attend. She crocheted all eight of us girls a tablecloth, doilies, and snowflakes to hang on our trees. She also crocheted a beautiful wall hanging of the Lord's Supper. Mom was a good gentle person who rarely said anything bad about anyone.

One day my Dad said he noticed that Mom was having a hard time remembering and getting things mixed up. It wasn't like she would forget where she put keys or what she went into a room for. This was different. Over time it seemed to get worse.

My Dad passed away in his sleep one night at the age of 90. She thought he was just sleeping from his nap yet. Finally, she called my brother. This all took a toll on her.

After that, my siblings and I took turns staying with Mom at her home to care for her 24/7. She was 89. We noticed her memory was getting worse. She loved to play the card game, Rook. She had learned to play as a child. We played with her most every day, but eventually noticed she was having problems playing too.

I, and another sibling, took Mom to a specialist where she was tested for dementia. A brain scan revealed there was shrinkage in the front of her brain which affected her memory and planning. She did not have Alzheimer's, but was diagnosed with dementia. Mom was put on Aricept.

She always knew who we were, but sometimes got mixed up due to she was also legally blind due to her macular degeneration. She said she could tell us by our voices and our silhouette.

MEMORIES OF MOM

My sweet mother, who rarely said anything bad about anyone, started to accuse people of stealing and would imagine there were strangers outside and she would become very frightened. We never left her alone and as I said we took care of her 24/7. We took care of her in her home for six years until it came to a point where we had to put Mom in an assisted living facility. It was hard, but we knew it had to be done as it was getting difficult to take care of her at her home anymore. Mom passed away at the age of 96. Seven years after my Dad passed.

—*Loving Daughter*

*Time with loved ones
is precious*

MY GRANDMOTHERS

Both of my biological grandmothers have Alzheimer's. My dad's mother was diagnosed a couple of months ago and my mom's mother was diagnosed almost 5 years ago. I also have an ex-neighbor who has Alzheimer's who now lives in an amazing nursing home near me. About 8 years ago, she and her husband "adopted" my sisters and I as their grandchildren, as she only has one grandson who is in his 30s. With all three of my beloved grandmothers, it has been a very sad, painful and bumpy ride for everyone involved, including caregivers and family members.

Regrettably, on my mom's side there have been too many arguments and legal disputes between my mom's siblings on where my Grandma Kraus should live: a nursing home, with my grandfather,

A LONELY JOURNEY

or with my aunt. Sadly, my grandfather isn't doing well, and has been living in a nursing home for a couple of months now, so he is unable to care for his wife. I can't even imagine the pain of not being able to live with your own wife. So for 3 years now my grandmother has been living with my aunt. I am very glad about that. I love all my aunts and uncles, but some of them wish her to be in a nursing home. I have nothing against nursing homes, but I believe that if there is a family member willing and able to be a caregiver, they should be able to. Some of my aunts and uncles don't understand how happy my grandmother is. Sometimes my aunt needs breaks, but otherwise she is a very good caregiver who keeps my grandmother happy and healthy. Both my mother and I think my grandmother is the happiest she has ever been.

One of the things Grandma Kraus does a lot is sing. Even though she is in the late stages of

Alzheimer's, remembering song lyrics is still very much possible for her. When there's a song on the radio, or if my aunt asks her to sing a specific song, she jumps right in beautifully. It just makes me love her so much more!

I can only hope my dad and his siblings are able to compromise better. But this is only the very beginning of Alzheimer's for my Grandma Ortner. She currently lives alone in a beautiful house out in the country. But has 14 kids, 6 of which live in her town and 2 on farms less than one mile away. At least one of her children visits her every single day. And every Christmas, Thanksgiving and Easter, along with family reunions, her birthday and Fourth of July, there are big parties and lots of fun. She may live alone and have a hard time remembering all 40 names of her grandchildren and great-grandchildren, but she is never lonely and she is certainly very loved.

A LONELY JOURNEY

Grandma N used to live across the street from my family and I and she and her husband "adopted" my sisters and I as their grandchildren. After her husband died at the age of 95, an extremely sad time for my whole family, my grandmother moved to a nursing home, and after about 3 years of living there, she was diagnosed with Alzheimer's She has 4 kids: 3 daughters, 1 son, and 1 grandson. Unfortunately, her son has since passed. two of her daughters and her one grandson all live far away, but her third daughter lives a couple miles from her nursing home, and visits my grandmother a lot. I try to visit her as much as I can also. Right now, she has a very good long term memory, but a bad short term memory. Last time I visited with her, she was telling me about her childhood, and even remembered what street she lived on when she was a child! How amazing is that? It makes me tear up just thinking about it.

One thing that has changed about me since my mom's mother was diagnosed with Alzheimer's my 8th grade year, is how I look at life. I have always loved my family, grandparents, and friends, but I almost always took them for granted. Now, with my grandmothers slowly deteriorating, I have realized I need to take a step back and enjoy what life has to offer. This disease is taking three extremely precious people from my life, and never before did I think that I would be so determined to make my last few years left with them on this earth worth it.

Something I have learned about my community and family is how committed everyone is on finding a cure or prevention for Alzheimer's. Finding a cure or prevention for Alzheimer's is one of the few things I have witnessed that everyone can agree on, that everyone is seeing eye to eye on. Being a caregiver or a loved one who has to cope with Alzheimer's and finding a cure or prevention

A LONELY JOURNEY

is really hard, but of what I have seen, no one has given up yet. It really is amazing to see that.

About 5 months ago, my family and I took part in an Alzheimer's Awareness walk in Marshfield, a city in the middle of Wisconsin. It was really cool to see hundreds of other people walking alongside me with the same goal as everyone else: to end this horrible disease we call Alzheimer's. Alzheimer's is the seventh leading cause of death in the United States. It affected 5.3 million people over the age of 65 and 200,000 people under the age of 65 in 2017; of those 5.3 million people, three of them were my grandmothers. Even after my grandmothers pass on, I will do everything in my power to end Alzheimer's, whether that be donating to research, joining a club in college, or taking part in more awareness walks. I just love them too much not to do all that. All three of my grandmothers mean so much to me. —*Gretchen* © *2018*

MY HEROES

When I heard about this project, I just had to be a part of this. I am not a caregiver for family members, but I do take care of residents who certainly feel like family.

I want you to know that I choose to work with dementia residents. I enjoy it and feel it does take a special person to care for loved ones with dementia. That is why I have the highest regard for you the caregivers at home as well as the caregivers who have entrusted your loved ones to me to care for.

I know how hard it is. I cannot imagine being in your shoes with a 24/7 shift. As much as I enjoy working with my residents, I have to admit I also enjoy going home to a good night's rest, which is something I know is a luxury for 24/7 caregivers.

At work, I have other caregivers to assist me. Again, this is something that 24/7 caregivers do not have the luxury of. You are my heroes!

Many family members are reluctant to have their loved ones in a care facility. Each person has their own reasons for wanting to keep their loved ones at home.

I do want you to know that there are so many good caring staff that will take care of your loved one. Care facilities will work with you on how you want your loved one to be cared for. Your loved one's likes and dislikes.

The stigma of nursing homes has changes so much over the years. Care facilities are similar to senior retirement villages. So many activities and opportunities. Some I have seen even have the feel of a luxurious resort.

I have seen caregivers stressed to the point that they have sacrificed their own health. I am sure you have heard it many times that if you don't take care of yourself how can you take care of anyone else. Your loved one is counting on you.

My purpose here is just to put your mind at ease that if life gets to the point that you feel you need more help with your loved one, don't feel guilty. In looking back, you most likely will feel it was the best decision you made for both you and your loved one.

Your loved one will still be yours to love and you will still be the caregiver, but you will have others to help meet your loved one's daily needs. Help so you can enjoy just being their wife, husband, daughter, son, niece or nephew etc.

Again, you are all my heroes!

—An Admirer

A LONELY JOURNEY

And as a caregiver,
sometimes I get it right

MY JOURNEY

In April of 2017, I found myself in East Jerusalem with my ex-husband, Dean, age 70, who has Alzheimer's. We had traveled from Chicago, now carrying our belongings in our backpacks, many hours without sleep. In search of a bus to Ramallah in the West Bank, 12 miles north, we had been dropped off in a large parking lot with several old school busses and about 50 people, many of whom seemed to be waiting for a bus to Ramallah. My 3 month study of Arabic on the internet thru the Appleton library proved completely inadequate, but one thing was clear, busses did not run on any set schedule. I had time to reflect on events that had brought me to that point.

Dean was diagnosed in 2014 and was devastated

at the loss of his ability to travel alone. We have been friends for over 50 years, married for 16 of those early years, no children, no close family ties. His greatest joy was traveling alone in third world countries for months at a time, with only a backpack full of more cameras than clothes. He had done this for over 25 years. I was inclined to stay close to home.

He had never been to Palestine, and when I discovered in *Backpacker* magazine that a new long-distance hiking trail was now open in the West Bank, an idea was planted in my mind: one last adventure for the photographer, if only I could learn how to do overseas travel. I own a computer, but before this had used it only for e-mail. Being part of a tour was out of the question—Dean insisted it must be his kind of travel, without a set itinerary or reservations. We compromised. I had reserved a room at a low budget hostel in Ramallah for the first night and a room in Jerusalem for the last night, leaving 13 days to wander in the wilderness.

Back in Jerusalem that first day, we eventually shared a cab with a young German with purple hair, changed cabs at the checkpoint 5 miles north, and made it into the city of Ramallah, only to find out that the address for our hostel was unfamiliar to our driver. We were dropped off in the general neighborhood and left to wander and ask, over and over, until we finally found it by mid-afternoon. It was left up to me to figure out how we were going to eat.

I learned very quickly that reservations were in fact required from one hostel to another. Lucky for me, the owners of each place were quite willing to help me find another in the next town and direct us to find a shared taxi. Dean was overjoyed to be in the midst of another culture, but couldn't help me with any part of it. As my stress mounted, the challenge was to be in right relationship with him, to behave lovingly, patiently, and kindly.

A few weeks before leaving on the trip I recall a conversation with a friend in which I expressed my hopes of meeting that challenge. I had imagined a movie in which the wife struggles with the responsibilities of the overseas adventure while the husband struggles with dementia. In my movie she rises to the occasion and love overcomes all frustrations, etc. I'm about to play the role of the wife and give an academy award winning performance.

Let me tell you what really happened. Dean was grateful that I had packed for him and I had organized his meds and toothbrush in each room as we went along. But then he moved stuff around arbitrarily, resulting in my frequent irritation, freely expressed, at having to re-organize and show him which was HIS toothbrush, HIS towel, and now it's time to move out and he tries to put his pack on upside down, spilling the contents on the floor.

He carries a heavy camera bag with an outdated digital camera for which he has brought the wrong memory card. We walk big city streets looking for a camera store, but everyone else seems to be using smartphones for their photos. Instead, he shoots with a tiny film camera that he brought for backup, capturing colorful urban scenes of murals and people, only to discover later that his film is black and white. In dealing with these setbacks I'm able to offer sympathy without reinforcing his feelings of inadequacy.

But I screw up again at the next hostel. We found ourselves in a luxurious, clean spacious room with a PRIVATE bath. Dean went for the shower first. Coming out, he raved about the warm water, but said now there was water all over the bathroom floor. It was like traveling with a six year old.

"Why didn't you use the shower curtain?" "What shower curtain? Oh, that's the shower curtain?" I had managed to humiliate him further.

Every time we left the familiarity of our various hostels to venture out, I had to learn how to find it again. Dean was lost as soon as we rounded the first corner.

It was heartbreaking for me to see Dean bear these humiliations with disappointment, brave acceptance, and even humor. It was strange to be with him one minute when he couldn't possibly locate his underwear and then listen to him converse so intelligently with a university professor over breakfast. Only once did he express his anger at me for treating him like a child and he was quick to forgive after I apologized.

At some point during the trip he began to "recognize" places that he claimed to have visited before. A hiking trail in the ancient land of Samaria, a café, a school, even a hostel in a small desert town outside of Jericho. He had been there before—why, he had stayed in a single room just down the hall! This irritated me to no end and I foolishly tried to convince him how mistaken he was. I fell way short of the model of the wife in the movie as we fought over this. My rational arguments couldn't compete with his certainty of his own memories.

I learned too late to just go along with it. What took so long? My own ego wanted credit for choosing a country with a different culture that he hadn't been to. I suppose I wanted more thanks for giving him this unique gift. But, of course, he didn't need the additional humiliation of being proven wrong.

There were times when the scenes of the imaginary movie did live up to my hopes. As darkness fell each evening around 7:00 p.m., we retreated to our room with nothing to do. Dean can no longer read for enjoyment because he can't hold the thread of the story from one page or chapter to the next. But for some reason he can listen to a story, a few chapters each night, and enjoy it. I became the reader for us both.

There was also discussion, conversations recalling the college days, places we had lived, jobs, interesting people we had known and, finally, some frank talk about the disease, even what to expect in the future. Feeling safe enough with each other to face the difficult reality.

Since that trip nearly a year ago, Dean speaks often of traveling again, trying to convince me of how much I'd love India or South Africa. I don't know whether it's kinder to nip the idea in the bud or let him hold on to the hope, while I'm thinking, "no way." Mostly, I suggest something easier, like renting a cottage on a Caribbean island, but he's not interested in anything as tame as that.

The disease progresses. He loses his phone, his keys, even large items like the two humidifiers he had last winter. He talks about finishing and using the darkroom in the basement even though he no longer knows how to mix the chemicals. His meds usually sit out on the kitchen counter, but once he was distraught when they had disappeared. Eventually I found them tucked away with the cereal boxes. At least 10 cereal boxes, stored in two different cupboards.

He slows down the rate of the disease's progression by regular, lengthy exercise at a fitness center five days a week and by using the maximum level of medication the doctor can prescribe. He remembers to take it most of the time.

I continue to look for the right balance between my part time job as caregiver and maintaining my own life. I check on him every other day, do all his finances, drive him to appointments (he still drives to a few familiar places), and spend social time with him at least once a week. I still fall short of the person I want to be when I'm with him. Sometimes because I speak too quickly and share thoughts better left unsaid. Sometimes I just don't know what the best response should be. And sometimes, once in a while, I get it right.

—Barbara Hoffman © 2018

MY LIFE AS A CAREGIVER

I feel I have always been a kind giving person so becoming a caregiver for my husband, Joe, was a task I was willingly accepting. Even at this point in our lives, I cannot imagine life without him.

Joe eventually became unable to communicate well and then friends and family slowly stopped their visits and became busy with their own lives. I am sure it was depressing for them to visit us as we had no great stories to share, but yet it was such a blessing for us to hear about their daily activities.

I love Joe dearly, but I find the role of a caregiver can be very difficult and lonely. I was really down one day and so I began to start counting my blessings to cheer myself up.

At the top of my list was the fact that Joe was still

with me. I can still sing or hum his favorite songs for him. I can still hold his hand. He may not be able to communicate well with me, but there is so much that I can still do for him. Things that I know he used to enjoy such as going for rides. I always said he should have been a truck driver.

Dementia is not on my list of blessings, but in some ways it brought us closer together. He is dependent on me and yet he brings happiness to me each day that I still have him. I choose my life as being his caregiver over not having Joe in my life.

When I feel sorry for myself, I stop to think just how horrible it must be for Joe. I have much to be thankful for and even though Joe isn't the companion he used to be, he is still here with me and I count that as one of my greatest blessings.

It may be easier to count the negatives, but I prefer the challenge of counting my blessings instead. I pray that you too will find the blessings to count in your life as a caregiver.

—Anonymous

A Mother's Love

MY SON'S CAREGIVER

I would think parents never think about becoming their son's caregiver. I know I never did. Sure I worried about car accidents, especially when he was a teenager, but dementia? Never.

His wife had just filed for divorce, so my son moved in with me. I saw some signs, but he was in a stressful situation and I put the blame on the pending divorce. I now wonder if that is why she filed for divorce. We have no contact so I will probably never know. In some ways, I can't blame her, but she took the easy way out. So, now I care for my son with a diagnosis of early onset dementia.

I have always wanted grandchildren, but now I am thankful he never had children. It is hard enough for me to see him struggle. He is an only child. I am divorced myself for too many years to count and his father has not had anything to do with him as well. So I am my son's caregiver.

There are days that it is hard to love him and there are days it is hard to love myself. I am never abusive physically or verbally with him, but there are days that I feel I could have been a better caregiver, a better mother. I have learned it is hard to be a mother and a caregiver.

I feel like a drill sergeant always telling him what he needs to do. Take a shower. Eat your food. Get dressed. Turn the TV down. Go to bed.

I find it is somewhat difficult to take him in public as he says inappropriate things about people and forgets how loud he talks and that they can hear him.

I know the day will come when I will have to let others care for him. The mother in me wants to care for him as long as I can at home. I hope when I can no longer care for him, that our relationship will return to the loving mother-son relationship that we had before.

—Love Mom

*Human nature needs
a sense of purpose*

SENSE OF PURPOSE

As strange as it sounds, being a dementia caregiver for a loved one, gives me a sense of purpose. I often wonder what would I be doing if I wasn't caring for him, especially at my age.

Having him to care for gives me a reason to get up, a reason to cook and clean. I know it sounds strange. It is not always easy, but it fills my day. In his own way, he keeps me company and makes me feel loved most days.

I realize, some day, we will no longer be together. So I wonder if he goes first, what then will be my sense of purpose. We have been together for so long and even before his dementia he was my sense of purpose as my spouse.

How will life change for me and what will I do

with my life. I worry. I worry too much. I do feel I have to be ready and plan for what is to come after I fulfil my purpose as his caregiver.

Recently, a thought came to me that my next sense of purpose may be to mentor other caregivers and share my experiences and suggestions to help them. This is something I will definitely check into when the time comes. I hope many of you will also look at mentoring as there certainly is a need.

—Anonymous

SOME DAYS

Honestly, SOME days I feel:

    Alone

    Confused

    Angry

    Bitter

    Depressed

    Unloved

    Isolated

    Tired

    Exhausted

    Under Appreciated

    Trapped

    Like Screaming

And I hope when this is all over there will be enough pieces left to put me back together again.

Fortunately MOST days I do, honestly, feel:

> Successful
>
> Driven
>
> Renewed
>
> Loved
>
> Supported
>
> Powerful
>
> Energized
>
> Understood
>
> In Charge
>
> Appreciated

Most days, I feel like I can do anything. I do work hard to keep my spirits up. I am a believer in daily prayer. It is to my advantage to be in a positive mood and have patience. If my patience is in check, then the days goes quite well. If my patience is low, then nothing seems to go right. I will admit it took me a bit to realize the control I actually have on how my days goes. It took practice on my part.

Lots of prayer and lots of patience.

I had to learn it does not matter if I am right. The only place arguing gets me is angry and upset. Yes, there are times when I cannot let him be right, but I have learned diverting his attention usually helps with those situations.

At this point, my good days as a caregiver outweigh my bad days. I hope and pray this will continue as times get harder.

—*Anonymous*

Caregivers are never alone

SUPPORT

Support is so important to me. I find great support in our local caregiver support functions. After I leave a support function such as a caregiver support group, I feel energized like I can take on the world again.

The next day or two that feeling wears off and again I feel down and back to my reality. I feel alone again.

Recently, I discovered there are online caregiver support groups such as on Facebook and at Caregiving.com and I am finding just reading the posts gives me the encouragement and support that I need daily to be a good caregiver.

Reading the posts helps me to realize that I am not alone and that there are so many others going through what I am experiencing as a memory caregiver.

Their advice is so valuable to me and sometimes I will give advice back. I am actually amazed at how much I have learned and how much experience I, myself, have to share that can help other caregivers.

So for your lonely days, I recommend you turn to a caregiving group on Facebook or go to Caregiving.com for support. It definitely helps me and I hope it helps you too.

—Anonymous

SUPPORT GROUPS ARE PRICELESS

When I was first told the title for this book, I thought how appropriate! I do feel alone most days even though I care for my husband in our home.

What gets me through each day, in addition to God and my faith, is the small monthly support group I attend. We are all memory caregivers and bound by our common thirst for answers as we care for our loved ones.

Wondering if you have a memory support group in your area? Search the internet for caregiver support programs in your area, ask your medical professionals or call your County Health and Family Services Office, or your pastor for starters.

If you cannot find a memory support group in

your area, start one! I did! Our group meets once a month in the early afternoon at a local restaurant for coffee and some even order dessert. It is a different mix each time depending on who is able to attend.

This group is priceless to me as there is such a wealth of knowledge among these amazing caregivers. It helps me see what my future may be and I get insight into how to handle current and future situations based on the first hand experiences that they share.

Some loved ones have passed, but the caregivers still join us and their input is still valuable especially as the journey is nearing the end for our loved ones. They also provide encouragement for us that life does go on for caregivers after the loved one passes.

I find by attending these monthly groups that I am refreshed for the month. I also find I don't burden others outside the group with my caregiver issues, which they don't usually understand anyway, and that allows my conversations with them to be about other topics. It seems like before this group, I would unload on anyone that would listen. Yes, sometimes even strangers.

This group is so wonderful and priceless! Only they can truly understand what I am going through as a memory caregiver. We share, we laugh and sometimes we get tears in our eyes, but we support each other as only memory caregivers can.

You may think you don't have time, but this is something that is very important and enjoyable for your own well being and you will be glad you joined.

Join a group today!

—Anonymous

*Education is important
for any disease*

THE D WORD

The dreaded "D" word. What stigma that word holds. Dementia is so misunderstood by society. You would think dementia was contagious by the way society reacts to the word.

I get that no one would want dementia, but the truth is that dementia is a disease. Dementia is not a mental illness which, by the way, is not contagious either.

Educating the world about dementia would be my greatest wish at this moment. Why do family and friends flee when they hear the D word? Why do they react differently than a broken leg or even cancer? My theory, and I suspect I am right, is the lack of education about dementia.

When a loved one has dementia, what they and the caregiver need more than anything is your support and understanding. Knowing that you have their back and that you are there for them no matter what.

Caregiving can make the caregiver feel isololated. Just knowing that you thought about them can bring a warm feeling and a smile to most caregivers. Having a get together? Invite them. Don't just assume they cannot make it. Let the caregiver make that decision. Even if they were not able to make it the last five times. This time may be the day that works out and they will both attend! To not be invited, makes any person feel alone.

I know this is short and sweet, but I hope if you are one of those who fear the word dementia that you will realize it is not contagious and the caregiver needs your love and support in whatever way you can give it.

It is not a glamorous journey, but you can make the journey easier for the caregiver with your love and support.

What can you do for a caregiver today?

—Fearless

A LONELY JOURNEY

*Life sometimes takes
unexpected twists and turns*

THIS IS NOT THE RETIREMENT WE PLANNED

I admit I feel guilty saying, this is not the retirement we planned, but Rob and I had saved and planned over the last 30 years for our dream retirement.

We were so excited when we finally made the decision to take the plunge and retire. There were so many plans to finalize and loose strings to tie before the big day.

Our dreams were only months away and we would talk excitedly about all our future travel plans to exotic places. It was an exciting time in preparing for our retirement.

Two months before the big day, Rob had some strange behavior. He woke up one weekend and didn't seem to know where he was and at first even looked at me strangely. Rob willingly agreed to have some tests performed.

The results were truly unexpected. Rob was in the early stages of dementia. Doctors could not tell us what the future would hold or how quickly the disease would take over Rob's cognitive abilities.

I was extremely resentful. This was not in our retirement plans. Our retirement was so close. Why now? I was resentful about the dementia diagnosis and found myself resentful to Rob as well for changing our retirement plans.

For the next few months, I could not bring myself to accept this was really happening to me. I wasn't even thinking about Rob and how this news was affecting him. I was only thinking about myself and how it was affecting my retirement and my life.

I am sure Rob would tell you I was acting like a spoiled child. I was.

I have since come to accept our retirement as it is. We are still able to be together more and we are still able to do fun things and even travel. Our social life is a bit quieter, yet in some ways that is nice too. I think we were actually living life at too fast a pace and this has helped us to slow down and enjoy life and to appreciate each other more.

I am grateful for this opportunity to share as it really helped me to reflect on our journey and allowed me to really look at my feelings. I am not angry with Rob. I am angry at the disease. Rob never asked for this nor did he do anything to cause it or deserve it.

I am sure as caregivers we go through numerous stages and I feel I am about to leave the angry stage and hopefully going into the acceptance stage and whatever stages come after that. I now plan to just enjoy the time I have with Rob. I do love him so!

— "Rob's" Loving Wife

A LONELY JOURNEY

Dementia is a hard
word to hear

TIME STOOD STILL

I know there are so many worse things in this world than dementia. I know there were so many worse things the doctor could have told us that day. I know it wasn't easy for the doctor to tell us.

I feel bad looking back at how I reacted. The doctor said I had a normal reaction, but I think he was being polite. The moment I heard the word dementia, I just froze. Time suddenly stood still and I am not sure I heard another word after that. My head was spinning with a million questions and yet not one of those questions would come out of my mouth.

What do we do next? Is there a cure? How far along is it? Can I keep him at home? Should I keep him at home? What are the medications? How much time do we have? How did he get this? Is it contagious? Is it hereditary? Are you sure? Is it Alzheimer's? What can I expect? Someone, please wake me up from this nightmare!

I felt so helpless. To be honest, I think I felt more sorry for myself than my husband. What a burden I was about to take on.

It took a few days, before either one of us could really talk about it. He was so much more accepting of the news than I was or so he pretended to be. I was scared. Scared of my future. Scared of his future.

I vowed that I would do my best to care for him at home, but he made me promise that if it ever became too much that I would consider some type of placement for him. He said he didn't want me to resent him and wanted me to just have time to be his wife and best friend and not be burdened with tasks that others could be doing instead of me.

How thoughtful of him to think of me.

My husband is slipping away slowly. So slowly that I think sometimes I don't notice the change. I am told that can change and in the future I may see big changes from day to day. There are days when he seems fine and then my hopes, that the doctors were wrong, are dashed as we go back into the so-called bad days.

I don't like to compare dementia to other diseases or illnesses, but I do like to think that things could be worse. As tough as it is and is going to be, so I am told, I do try to find a bright side to all this. It is hard to make sense out of everything, but I do my best for my loving and thoughtful husband.

—One Day at a Time

Traveling can be a challenge for both the loved one and the caregiver

TRAVELING

My husband has always been a big traveler. You could say he lived for family trips. Unfortunately, after dementia came into our lives, we found traveling was no longer the best idea for my husband.

His now lack of patience make it difficult for him to stand in long lines and sometimes even short lines. He no longer seems to have a tolerance for others. Especially, if he feels someone is talking too loud or too much. He usually likes to let them know or at least announces it loudly to anyone within hearing distance. Luckily, my friendly smile seems to defuse the situations.

I have heard this behavior comes from the fact that dementia will take away the filters that we all supposedly have. Knowing what to say and not say, at least publicly. This lack of filters allows him to give his opinion quite freely in many situations. Some days, I wish I had his lack of filters instead of being as polite as I am.

When traveling now just for our day trips, I do have to watch him much more closely. Very much like I would a young child. He can become fascinated with something or someone and if I don't keep my eye on him, he will quickly disappear into a crowd of people or lag behind. He never was a person who liked to hold hands for some reason. Sometimes I will ask to hold his arm to help guide him suggesting that I needed his arm to lean on, but that doesn't seem to suit him either.

It is nice that now many places have a family restroom. Although he doesn't want me to go in with him, it does allow me to be outside the door and knock if I start to worry about him taking too long. I have had too many occasions where I had to ask other men to check to see if he was still in the men's restroom when he would linger too long.

As you can imagine, I cannot rely on him to help me find a location or street etc. Thankfully at this point, if I need to leave him for a few moments, I am still able to tell him to sit and stay there until I return. He will not go into a family restroom with me even if I am the one in need. Very taboo for him for some reason. I think perhaps a generational thing.

He feels a need to always have a twenty dollar bill in his wallet. He can have a ten and two fives, but to him that is not twenty dollars. He is eager to give me whatever is in his wallet in exchange for a twenty dollar bill. It makes him smile. Should he lose the twenty dollars, to me it is such a small price to pay to see him happy and to see him smile. I do have a list of names and phone numbers in his

A LONELY JOURNEY

wallet as well, just in case I should ever lose track of him.

We still travel. Just not as far and not as long. I have learned to make adjustments so we can still enjoy a bit of traveling. It is good for me and good for him. At least for now.

—Anonymous

WHAT I HAVE LEARNED

I have learned so much about this disease in the past seven years and yet there seems to be so much more to learn as we continue our journey.

Please note these lessons have not been written in any particular order of importance. I listed them as they came to mind. Also, since some of these topics do overlap, please forgive me if I repeat myself.

TIME FRAME— I have learned that each person is affected differently and yet there are similarities. Each person moves through the journey at their own pace. I am not aware that there is any rhyme or reason as to the pace.

PATIENCE—As a caregiver, I have learned most importantly to be patient with my loved one as well as myself. I am sure you have heard this many times, but it is important.

NAPS—I have found naps are so important for my husband. His naps, as well as his sleep at night, profoundly affect his mood and dictates if we have a bad day or a good day. Although sleep is important for everyone, I have noticed sleep deprivation really affects those with dementia to a higher degree than the average person. From what I understand naps are important for his moods because his mind has to work so much harder to maneuver his day even to simply think of the correct word to express himself.

When I finally stopped fighting his three naps a day, I found we both had a better day. Each nap gives me at least an hour to myself to catch up on household chores or read the paper or enjoy a cup of coffee while addressing some emails or perhaps maybe a little nap myself. In turn, he wakes up somewhat rejuvenated and in a better mood until he needs to nap again.

LARGE GROUPS—I have learned large groups are difficult for my husband. I even select what church service we will attend based on what service I feel may have the least attendance. For some reason, he now always has to sit in the back of the church near the door as well. Things have changed, but I do what I have to so he feels comfortable and so we both have a good experience.

I do notice with larger groups he will hang off to the side and not involve himself. I then try to involve him and if that doesn't work then I ask if he would like to go home and he usually chooses that we leave.

DECISIONS—Making decisions seems to be hard. Choosing what to order at a restaurant can be overwhelming. What to wear many times becomes the same favorite shirt.

FINANCIAL MATTERS—For obvious reasons,

financial matters were the first thing I had to take over completely myself. Before we had a diagnosis, I was hearing reports of him leaving large tips for a cup of coffee. I also learned he was in the process of purchasing land which he was going to turn into a park. Luckily, I was able to get us out of that deal.

Now he is content as long as he has some ones in his wallet. I am okay with that. Someday he may wander off and I may be happy that he has a few dollars in his wallet.

CONTACT INFORMATION—Because I do worry about him eventually wandering, I have put a list of contact names and phone numbers in his wallet.

LOCKING DOORS—At night, I always double check to see that the doors are locked and any outside lights are off. We were having issues where he would also be checking the doors, however, he was unlocking them after I locked them. Now, I do the final locking of the doors after he goes to sleep.

RELIGION—I feel my husband has become more spiritual. I know my faith has certainly been challenged and has grown as a result of my husband's dementia. Although he doesn't talk about it, I am sure he has to be scared of the future to some degree.

DIET—His diet has been quite interesting actually. He seems to have developed a sweet tooth that is insatiable. It is difficult for me to take him into a grocery store as he wants to fill the cart up with cookies and candy. In the past, I tried to reason with him, which usually made a scene, but I have learned the best thing to do is to secretly put them back on a shelf as we continue our shopping.

I also find it interesting that his taste in food has changed. He was pretty much a meat and potato kind of guy. Strictly American cuisine. Now he enjoys Mexican food.

One day, in the grocery store, he grabbed a cantaloupe and put it in the cart. He has never enjoyed cantaloupe or watermelon and has even complained of the smell when I eat it. I asked him what he was going to do with the cantaloupe and he stated that he loves cantaloupe. So we bought it and he did, indeed, enjoy it and he now eats cantaloupe and watermelon. I am amazed.

FAMILY AND FRIENDS—It takes time for family and friends to adjust and to accept the diagnosis. Just as it did for me. By the time I finally told family and friends about the dementia, I was already in acceptance. So naturally, just hearing about the diagnosis they were in denial and needed some time to process the news as well.

Some family members and friends will never come around and will always be in denial about the diagnosis. I have offered the opportunity to family members who are in denial to come along to doctor appointments, but so far no one has accepted my offer.

HYGIENE—From what I hear from other caregivers, I am fortunate that my husband still keeps up on his hygiene. Some days he does forget and, of course, his body odor gives him away. I then will ask him if he thinks he should take a shower. Notice I said ask, not tell him to take a shower. I find asking works much better than telling him to do something. By my asking, it makes him feel as he made the decision to take a shower.

We are still working on the shaving as he usually cuts himself. Trying different shavers, but at this point he refuses to use an electric shaver.

Every day he douses himself in spray-on deodorant. I have shown him how he doesn't have to use that much, but he continues to do it his way. I also am still suggesting a roll on deodorant, but so far he isn't interested. Picking my battles!

LAUGHTER IS CHEAP MEDICINE—Time for laughter is important in the life of a caregiver as well as the loved one. I have learned I can sometimes diffuse a tense situation by adding humor. So glad I learned this one!

IT IS NOT IMPORTANT TO BE RIGHT—No matter how wrong my husband may be, it is not important that I be right. He truly believes that he is right and nothing will convince him otherwise. It cost me nothing to let him be right, unless of course it would cause him harm, so I do my best to remember to back off and let him be right. As they say, "Pick your battles!"

GOOD DAYS AND BAD DAYS—I quickly learned there are good days and bad days. I have not been able to determine what dictates a bad day or a good day. Whenever I think I have it figured out my theory proves me wrong.

I do feel adequate sleep definitely contributes to

his good days, as it does to mine or anyone for that matter, including naps as he needs them. Adequate sleep is extremely important for a good day.

I often wonder about how diet affects his moods, but so far that has been difficult for me to narrow anything down due to so many variables. I have read studies regarding the benefits of an ounce of dark chocolate or one glass of red wine for cognitive health, but again I have no proof. I do offer him dark chocolate, but he is not fond of wine.

LESS IS MORE—I find it is important that I make sure his schedule is not overly stimulating. I try to keep it to one activity per day and most importantly to include days without activities as well each week.

TAKE TIME FOR ME—It was difficult in the beginning to remember to take time for myself. I was so busy trying to learn everything I could about dementia and running to doctor appointments.

Basically, just making sure I was doing everything possible to help my husband and making sure no piece of information was falling through the cracks.

After about a year, I realized taking care of myself is very, very important. You can't take care of someone if you are not taking care of yourself first is great advice. At this point, I realized how tired I really was.

As I looked back over the past year, I couldn't believe how far we had come and how much I had learned from scouring the internet and reading books. It was now time to start taking care of myself as well as my husband.

I began getting out for short visits with friends over coffee or lunch. It felt good. My world had been so small with just my husband and myself. It felt good to have other things to think about other than dementia. I felt he enjoyed hearing some of the news I would come back and share with him as well. This little bit of time for myself was precious to both of us. It truly makes me a better caregiver.

HUG YOURSELF—Take time to compliment and hug yourself for the fantastic job you are doing. Don't let negative self-talk bring you down. None of us are perfect and none of us have all the answers. So right now, wrap your arms around yourself and hug yourself until you have to let go! You deserve it more than you know! You are awesome!

HIPPA—This one is a big one! I learned the hard way that it is so important to have those Release of Information forms signed at ALL the doctors' offices and insurance companies. As luck would have it, we were going through the diagnosis process just as HIPAA (Health Insurance Portability and Accountability Act) was becoming law. My poor husband was being asked to sign so many forms that he was getting paranoid about signing anything.

We did have our Power of Attorney (POA) papers for both medical and financial completed years ago. Fortunately, our lawyer made the financial POA active immediately, but our medical POA papers have to be approved by two doctors to activate.

At this point, the doctors are reluctant to activate the medical POA. Since we have the Release of Information forms signed, we have not had any further issues. Our medical offices do require that we update these forms every year, so whenever we have an appointment, I ask if the form needs updating as I would hate to have one expire.

My husband does insist that I be in the room when he meets with his doctors which is huge for keeping me informed, but all decisions about medication changes are still legally his decision. Fortunately, his doctors are good at helping him make the best decision.

ADVOCACY IS IMPORTANT—I always trusted my doctors for the most part. The diagnosis part of our journey was hard. We were dealing with a lot of specialist who didn't know what was "normal" for my husband. I quickly learned that I needed to speak up even if the doctor did not appreciate it.

Since the specialist did not know my husband, I was getting feedback that he did not feel there were any issues especially with dementia. I have since learned that this is called "showboating" where the person can hold back the dementia. Dementia testing was completed and although he did not do well, he did well enough on the test to get a passing mark.

A year later, testing completed by another specialist confirmed a diagnosis of dementia. In defense of the first specialist, perhaps the disease wasn't progressed along enough at that time.

I am extremely active in all his appointments and care. I cannot rely on my husband to accurately tell me what was discussed at the appointment. Did I mention my husband believe he does not have dementia?

DENIAL—Cognitive diseases are challenging. If a person breaks their arm, of course, they want to see a doctor. If a person has a bad cold or sore throat, they ask to see a doctor. If a person is having memory issues, you hope they would ask to see a doctor.

I have heard of many cases where people with memory issues will recognize it and will ask for help especially in the early stages. My husband was not one of those people. To this day, he still denies that there are any issues with his memory. I, of course, do not argue with him as it does no good to argue about it.

I do find it interesting that in spite of my

husband's denial, he will still go to medical appointments for the dementia and is accepting of medication that is prescribed.

TOUCH—I find loving touching is important to my husband. I think it assures him that I do care and that I am here for the long haul. I benefit as well from the touching. It is human nature to touch and by touching to feel safe and loved.

There are days that he does not want to be touched and I respect that. I have learned to recognize the signs.

I AM AMAZING—I have learned that I am a very amazing person! I have endured situations and days that I never would have thought I could. I credit this strength to my faith in God. I cannot imagine how I would have gotten through any of this without God at my side. I am sure dementia has strengthened and tested my faith in many ways.

I have learned so much as a memory caregiver

A LONELY JOURNEY

for my husband and yet I feel I have so much more to learn as we continue our journey together.

—*A Bit Smarter*

WHAT I MISS MOST

I miss the old days: The laughter. The social life. Companionship. Going to movies. The traveling. The romance.

My husband was diagnosed with early onset. We are considered fairly young to be dealing with dementia which, of course, is why they call it early onset. I have also seen it referred to as younger onset on websites.

It is hard to see friends carry on with their normal lives as we sit by and watch. There is so much he is no longer able to participate in. Sometimes, I think he doesn't get involved due to depression regarding his situation, but he denies any depression.

Although I miss the old days, we somehow have adapted and found "our new normal," as they say. We make adjustments as needed such as we keep visits short as he tires easily. Traveling is now day or half-day trips. I seem to find laughter more easily than he does now and most times that seems to annoy him.

As much as I miss the old days, I realize I have to live in what is our new normal, as I really seem to have no choice. I have found chat groups and blogs give me comfort as well as ideas in how to cope with our new normal.

I have learned I have to take my clues from him and in order to keep peace, per say, I have to conform to his needs. As I indicated, this many times means cutting an enjoyable evening with friends short. We are so blessed to have such understanding friends that understand last minute cancellations and early departures.

Even though I miss the old days and envy our friends with their normal lives, I do prefer to be in the same "normal" as my husband.

—*Normal*

Dementia is not contagious

WHAT IS DEMENTIA

First, I do want to make it clear that I am not a medical professional. I am a caregiver of a loved one diagnosed with dementia.

What is dementia? I cannot give you medical advice or information, but I can tell you that dementia is not contagious. That is probably the main point that I wish to make clear in my submission.

I would guess, it is the lack of knowledge that puts fear in the minds of people who are ignorant as to what dementia truly is. Dementia is not a mental illness even though it affects the mind. Dementia is a disease.

I get extremely frustrated when people who do not understand what dementia is act as if it is contagious or who refer to it as a mental illness.

From my own experience as a caregiver, I see that the disease progresses slowly, but the pace of the disease seems to vary person to person. There seems to be similarities, yet differences from person to person.

Loved ones with dementia can still feel your presence. They can still enjoy listening to music. They can still enjoy the sound of a friendly voice. They can still enjoy your gentle touch. Depending on the stage of the disease, they can even have a conversation with you. I have found they love to talk about their childhood or raising their children or a hobby that made them happy.

I don't mean to preach, but I want everyone to know that my loved one doesn't deserve to be shunned as if she doesn't understand. If you have a question, don't ask me. Ask her. There may be a day she cannot answer, but for now ask her. Talk

WHAT IS DEMENTIA

to her. She is not contagious and she is not mentally ill. She has disease classified as dementia. For a fuller understanding about dementia, please check out the Alzheimers.org website.

—*All My Love*

*Poetry and music can be
soothing to the loved one
as well as the caregiver*

WHO IS LOOKING BACK AT ME?

I see her brown eyes fixed on mine
Who is looking back at me?
Is it you, O Lord, dwelling deep within
her bent and aging body held in catatonic pose?
Her eyes seek longingly, her lips cannot speak
I take her hand, a mild grasp in return, awareness
of a human connection, skin touching skin.
I look into her eyes and slowly pray
"Our Father, who art in heaven..."
Did I see her lips move in prayer? Is she recalling
something precious long lost in her fading memory?
Could this be, O Lord, a signpost on her slow, foggy
journey to Love's eternal embrace?

— Lenore Domers © 2009

A LONELY JOURNEY

The journey is easier if you travel with other caregivers

YOU ARE NOT ALONE

I remember in the beginning how alone I felt. I did not know anyone else whose spouse had been diagnosed with dementia, especially early onset.

To tell the truth, initially, I didn't even want to tell anyone about the diagnosis. It was very difficult when I eventually told our kids, his family, my family and eventually friends. Everyone seemed so stunned when they heard the news.

Even though it has been ten years, I still can't believe it. He has good days and bad days and those good days give you hope that the doctors are wrong, but the bad days remind you that the disease is still there.

I had to do a lot of research on my own. We lived in a very rural area and the resources were not there to help me locally. I feel things have greatly improved since then.

Maybe I feel things have improved just because I now know where the resources are, but in my opinion, society as a whole, has become so much more aware of dementia. It seems it takes time for society to understand and embrace a disease.

Many times it seems it takes a famous person such as President Ronald Reagan to bring the disease to the attention of the public, or even more locally former Governor Martin Schreiber who is a caregiver for his wife, Elaine.

If you are feeling alone, I strongly urge you to contact the Alzheimer's Association on their website for programs in your area. There are plenty of programs out there to help caregivers with the loneliness that caregivers often experience.

I am involved in caregivers share groups and the camaraderie and support is immeasurable.

You don't get strange looks when you share what you are currently going through as I often would get from friends and family when I would share. The group totally understands and most have also experienced it as well or soon will be experiencing it depending on how far the disease has progressed for their loved one.

Remember, you need to take care of yourself so you can take care of your loved one. Statistics show that caregivers who do not take care of themselves do not outlive their loved ones.

Call today and join a support group soon. Your loved one is counting on you to take care of yourself so you can take care of them.

You are NOT alone!

—A Friend

Thank you for this opportunity to be part of your journey

THANK YOU

I am honored and humbled to be trusted with compiling the sharing of these journeys to make this book possible. All credit goes to the amazing caregivers who were eager to share their journey.

This book is a compilation of untouched sharing as written in the caregivers' own words. Through this sharing, it is the hope that other caregivers will find comfort and that family members, friends, co-workers and employers will come to understand the journey of dementia caregivers.

I am confident that as a caregiver, family member, friend, co-worker or employer, you will find valuable information shared in this book.

Which journeys touched you the most? Which are your favorites? We would like to hear from

A LONELY JOURNEY

you. Contact us at www.JourneyPublish.com.

Although the journey seems lonely at times, caregivers are truly never really alone as shared in these amazing journeys.

—CC Thompson

AFTERWORD

Whether you are a caregiver, family member, friend, co-worker, employer, or medical provider, it is our hope that you were able to take away something from what these amazing caregivers have shared.

Please note The Alzheimer's Foundation of America Hotline is always there for you and is available 24/7 at 800-272-3900 to assist you with information or when you need someone to just listen.

Direct all medical and legal questions to your medical and legal professionals

DISCLAIMER

These journeys are written and shared by memory caregivers, in their own words, not by medical or legal professionals.

Any information shared in this book is not intended to be nor should it be interpreted as medical or legal advice.

Medical and legal questions or concerns should be directed to your medical and legal professionals.

*May you find comfort and
support in your journey*